The Gliding Flight

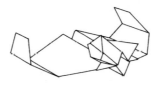

John M. Collins

The Gliding Flight

20 EXCELLENT FOLD AND FLY

PAPER AIRPLANES

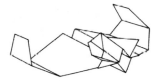

✈ TEN SPEED PRESS

BERKELEY, CALIFORNIA

1⊖

Ten Speed Press
Box 7123
Berkeley, CA 94707

Folding illustrations by the author
Flip-through animation and finished plane drawings by Marilyn Hill
Cartoons by Bill Mather
Cover design by Fifth Street Design
Text design by Nancy Austin
Typeset by Pamela Meyer

Library of Congress Cataloging-in-Publication Data
Collins, John.
    The gliding flight / by John Collins.
        p.   cm.
    ISBN 0-89815-313-1
    1. Paper airplanes. 2. Origami. I. Title.
TL778.C65 1989
745.592--dc20   89-33574
                                        CIP

First Printing, 1989

    2   3   4   5 -- 93   92   91   90

SPECIAL THANKS

To Professor Illan Kroo of Stanford University, the man with the answers.

To the cast and crew of the night shift in general. And in particular:

Midge A. for eagle eyes.

John G. for Thursday night encouragement.

Bob B. and Rob B. for displaying interest above and beyond the call of duty.

Dave G. for post production.

Jim G. for enduring endless strafing.

Lori for enthusiasm.

Gary, Pete, Mark, Bob, Syl, Suzanne, and Karl for shameless promotion.

Greg—one of my co-pilots and co-conspirators.

Danny—my other co-pilot, the man who single handedly lifted the Phoenix from the ashes.

And to my wife, who with the determination and grace of a proud single parent, is doing a fine job raising two boys—my son and me. I love you and thank you, Suzanne.

FOR MY SON
Sean Stephen Collins

CONTENTS

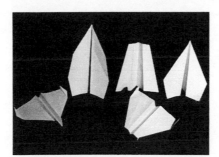

DARTS, page 23

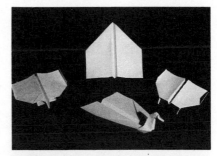

SPECIALTY INDOOR, page 117

GLIDERS, page 55

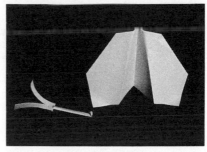

ACCESSORIES, page 135

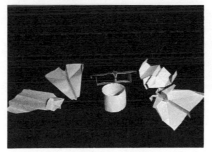

SPECIALTY INDOOR/OUTDOOR,
page 85

EXPANDED CONTENTS ▶

DARTS

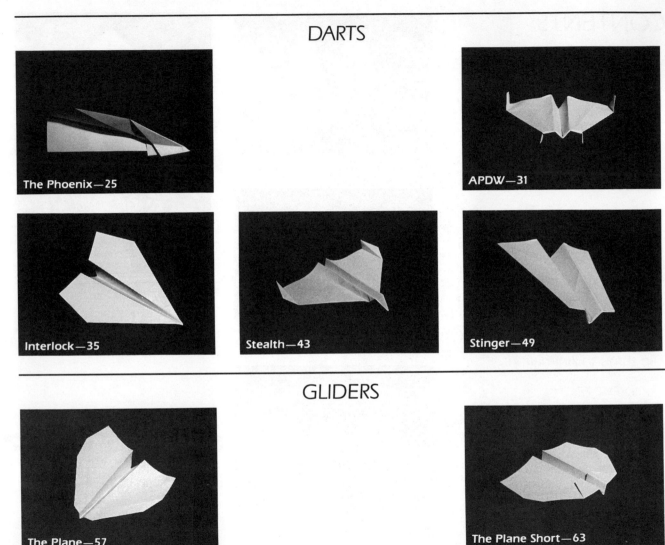

The Phoenix—25

APDW—31

Interlock—35

Stealth—43

Stinger—49

GLIDERS

The Plane—57

The Plane Short—63

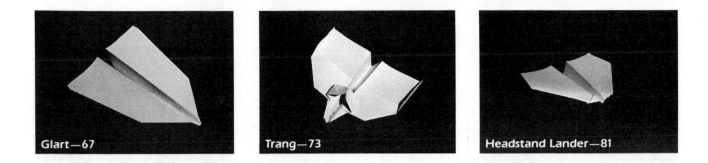

SPECIALTY INDOOR/OUTDOOR

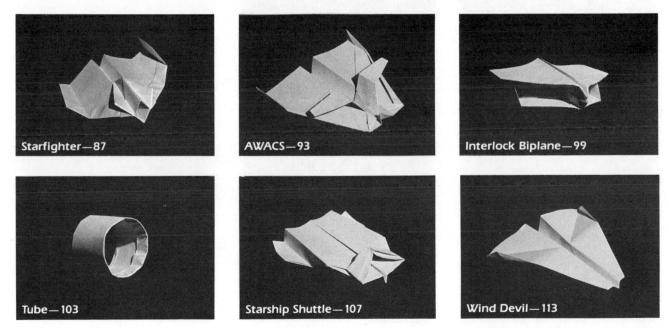

SPECIALTY INDOOR

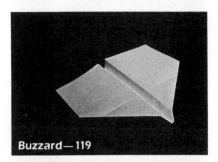

Buzzard—119

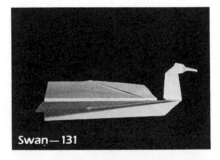

Twin Jet—123

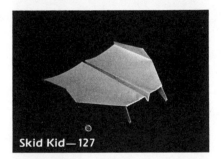

Skid Kid—127

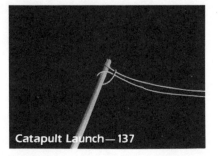

Swan—131

ACCESSORIES

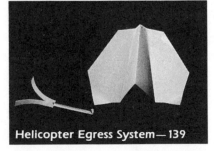

Catapult Launch—137

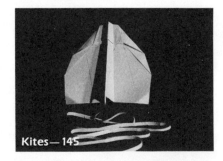

Helicopter Egress System—139

Kites—145

INTRODUCTION

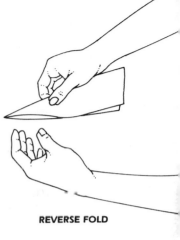

REVERSE FOLD

True flight is unobtainable. We learn to run like most land animals; first the fumbling steps, then straining for speed. We can learn to swim and enjoy the weightless motion in the water we seek in the sky. But we are not equipped to join the fanciful world of flight, even briefly.

Flying is a magical action that all ages stop to admire, be it the hovering of a hummingbird or the graceful climb of a 747 into the clouds. We cannot experience flight the way a bird or butterfly does, and must be assisted by technology to get into the air. Except in our dreams, human flight is always destined to be a vicarious experience.

A rectangle of paper is the low end of technology when it comes to flight. It is figuratively and literally the thinnest possible technological barrier between us and the air. A little added imagination can help you aloft and in an aircraft, climbing, diving, or banking into the wind.

Fold a piece of paper and join the realm of pure flight. If you can fold a straight edge, you can fly. I love flying these paper airplanes and watching them follow the winds and updrafts. I hope you will too.

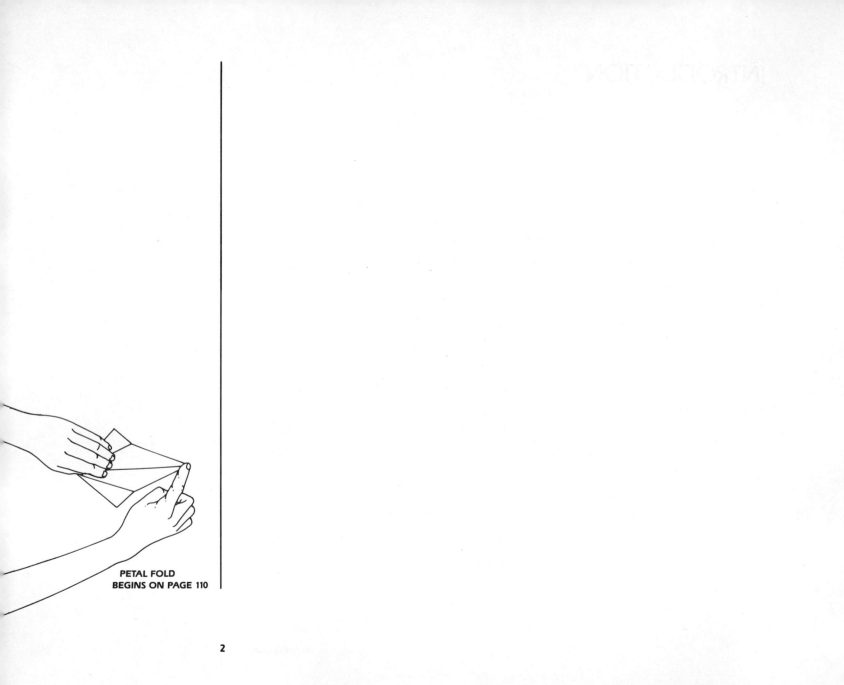

**PETAL FOLD
BEGINS ON PAGE 110**

Folding Instructions

Any 8½ by 11 sheet of copier or typewriter paper will work for these airplanes. My personal favorite is 20 pound copier paper that has been copied onto once. Most photocopiers have a heat process that stiffens the paper just a little, helping the sheet hold a crease.

Always fold accurately and crisply; this can't be stressed enough. Small errors in preliminary stages get amplified in the finished airplane. Sharp creases are easier to manipulate or reverse direction.

Look at the step you're on and the next step. This will show you what to fold and how it looks after folding. It's also important to remember that no matter how complicated the drawing looks, it boils down to valley folds and mountain folds.

A valley fold looks like a valley when viewed from above; a mountain fold looks like a mountain when viewed from above. When folding a single layer (like folding a page in half), a mountain fold is a diagramming convenience. It's easier to flip the paper face down, make a valley fold, and then flip the paper back to its original face-up position. This will create a mountain fold.

More complex moves—squashes, reverses, sinks, or petal folds—require manipulating more than one layer at a time. That's why I've provided a new way to learn them. The flip-through animation shows these moves actually happening. All you need to do is flip through the book where indicated in the table of contents and watch the action.

The animations should be thought of as the generic case. Squashes or reverses can look different when used in different ways. Similarly, I've invented several waterbomb-like bases. The waterbomb base in the animation shows the classic case. I've expanded the triangle to a trapezoid for the Stinger, shortened the top layer for the Interlock, and turned it upside down for the Headstand Lander.

RAT Folding

Avoid RAT (Right About There) folding unless indicated. Every fold made has a specific reference point. RAT folding will produce unrepeatable results. This is particularly important to remember when you use some of these ideas to start creating your own aircraft.

Good luck, and good flying.

Trimming and Flying

For FOLD AND FLY paper aircraft, the gap between theory and application is a thin one. Two things make a successful paper airplane: proper nose weight and correct trim. Since my designs are already well balanced, let's talk about trimming. There are two kinds of common problems. The SPLAT (Special Parameters Lacking Attention on Takeoff) throw and the OOPS (Obvious Operational Problem Syndrome) toss. Here's a SPLAT throw.

*Special Parameters
Lacking Attention
on Takeoff*

This particular problem can be solved by making an up elevator adjustment since the throw was a nose dive. Take a look at the following diagrams. You can correct for almost any variation of a SPLAT throw using these techniques.

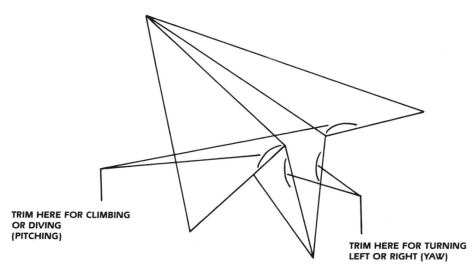

TRIM HERE FOR CLIMBING OR DIVING (PITCHING)

TRIM HERE FOR TURNING LEFT OR RIGHT (YAW)

Bend trailing edges the desired direction of travel—right to go right, etc. It's very easy to over correct, so make only small adjustments.

One more idea about trimming: high aspect ratio wings (wings with a greater span than length) are more sensitive to adjustment than lower aspect ratio wings. A dart-shaped plane will take more up elevator to correct a nose dive than a broad-wing glider.

Let me stress the need to check *dihedral angle*. Dihedral angle is the amount the wings are positioned above or below the horizontal. To check the dihedral angle, view the airplane from the nose or tail and observe the position-

DIHEDRAL ANGLE

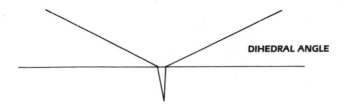

ing of the wings. They both should connect to the fuselage at the same angle. Symmetry is crucial. They should also be adjusted to the optimum angle for that particular airplane. The folding instructions will guide you.

Proper dihedral keeps the plane from rolling. If the plane gets rocked by a gust of wind to this attitude:

The left wing will generate more lift during that rolling motion and level the aircraft out. Why? Because an effective increase in the angle of attack of the left wing is caused by the rolling motion. More about angle of attack later.

Try this:

Fold a piece of paper in half and hold it as shown. Try moving it from side to side. See the natural resistance to the side to side movement? That's how dihedral angle provides stability.

Also remember that the airplane will flop open in flight. So add some dihedral angle to compensate for that amount of flop.

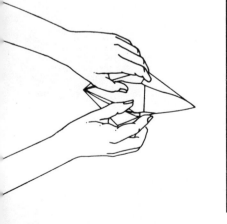

A flat dihedral in your hand can turn into negative dihedral in flight when the fuselage flops open.

*Obvious Operational
Problem Syndrome*

The OOPS toss requires you to examine your throwing technique.

The aircraft could be trimmed perfectly, but you could be releasing it wrong. Start with gentle releases to check your trim adjustments, and work your way toward faster flights. If the aircraft is gliding straight with a soft toss, chances are it's trimmed properly. If a harder throw makes it nose down (normal in a lot of planes), add some up elevator. But if a harder toss makes the airplane turn or roll suddenly, it's probably your throwing technique.

Always try for a controlled release with wings level. Release trajectory (this is the tough part) should be straight, like you're playing darts. Most people have to work on throwing technique, particularly for high speed launching.

Some other points to remember:

- Check the aircraft for overall symmetry. Dihedral angle, winglet attitude, leading edge sharpness, and trailing edge attitude (except where trimmed) all need to match closely from one wing to another.

- Hold the airplane close to the nose, particularly where there are the most layers of paper. This will be very close to the center of gravity and that's where you want to grab.

- Don't grip so hard as to bunch or warp the wing surface. Some planes are more sensitive to this than others.

- Control the throw and you can have consistent success.

Theory

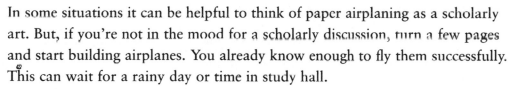

In some situations it can be helpful to think of paper airplaning as a scholarly art. But, if you're not in the mood for a scholarly discussion, turn a few pages and start building airplanes. You already know enough to fly them successfully. This can wait for a rainy day or time in study hall.

So, how do paper airplanes fly? First, let's talk about lift.

Curved wing surface will generate lift.

Look familiar? This is a conventional airfoil, developing lift using a curved surface to produce a curve in the airflow over the wing. The curving of the airflow is the important concept.

Think of the two outside airflow lines of this drawing as paths two runners must take when racing around an object. The runner below the wing runs a straight line from the front of the wing to the end. The runner above the wing must run a curve and hence run further. In order to finish even with the runner below, he must run faster along his route.

Daniel Bernoulli was a Swiss mathematician who studied how liquid behaved at different speeds. In 1738 he discovered that the pressure of a liquid falls as the speed increases. This idea is called Bernoulli's principle. It's because of Bernoulli's principle that the speeds of the two runners going around the wing are important.

The runner (or air) going over the wing has to go faster than the runner below. The faster the air moves, the lower the pressure over the wing. The air under the wing has a higher pressure because it's traveling slower. This difference in air pressures causes lift because the higher pressure under the wing pushes it toward the lower pressure.

Try this simple experiment. To demonstrate that a fast moving stream of air can create lift, hold a piece of paper so that most of it falls off the edge of a table. Blow a stream of air across the top of the table and over the sheet of paper. The sheet should lift into the airstream over the sheet.

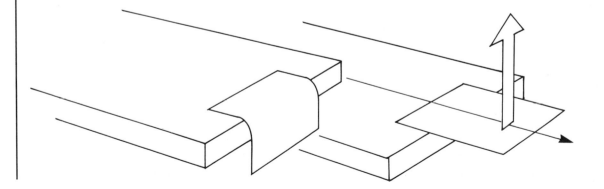

The drawing below is closer to how a paper airplane wing behaves—like a flat plate. Notice the plate angled up in front. That angle is called the *angle of attack*. In paper airplanes that is the critical characteristic.

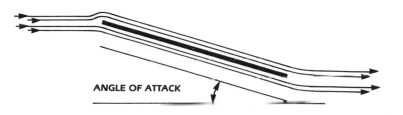

ANGLE OF ATTACK

Flat plate using angle of attack to generate lift.

Notice the air curving over the wing—faster moving air, lower pressure, and resulting lift. It's the same basic principle.

Too great an angle of attack causes stalling. The air can no longer curve around the leading edge smoothly. It separates from the wing surface and lift is lost.

Flat plates are less efficient than curved surfaces in terms of lift to drag, so you won't see them on conventional aircraft. However, today's fighter jets—F-14 or F-16—have wings that are curved on top and bottom. The curvature helps the wing slip through the air, but doesn't generate the kind of lifting force in the curved wing drawing. These planes rely on angle of attack to generate lift, similar to the way your paper airplanes will.

In flight there are four opposing forces. Lift opposes gravity, and thrust opposes drag. Take a look.

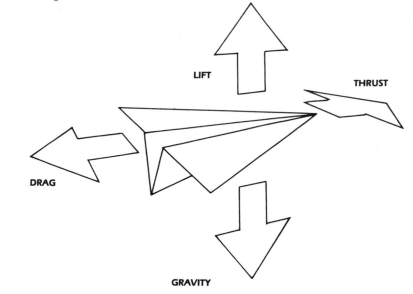

LIFT

THRUST

DRAG

GRAVITY

The center of lift is the point on the airplane that lift seems to be acting through. Center of lift can vary with changing airspeed.

The center of gravity on an aircraft is the point at which gravity seems to act through the craft. Picture an airplane suspended by a single thread. The point where the thread would need to be placed in order for the plane to balance perfectly would be the center of gravity.

On paper airplanes, the center of gravity needs to be just far enough forward as to coincide with the center of lift. If the center of lift is in front of or behind the center of gravity, the nose will pitch down or up respectively. Trim-

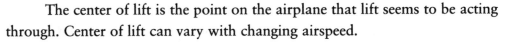

ming can compensate for slight mismatches of the center of gravity and the center of lift.

Thrust is initially supplied by you, the launching mechanism. Gravity constantly pulls the aircraft down, so if your plane points down, gravity will add to thrust instead of directly opposing lift. A crash can result, and it's not pretty.

Drag is the demon of the paper airplane world. Every time you add a trim adjustment to correct a flight problem, you add drag. Any surface not parallel to the flow of air adds drag. Since lift and thrust forces are very limited in the world

Drag demon

of paper flight, every effort should be made to reduce drag. Sharp creases and accurate folding will add time aloft to any design by reducing drag.

Once aloft, the aircraft can be made to rotate about the center of gravity by trimming.

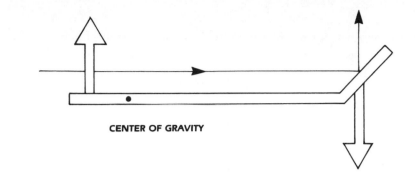

CENTER OF GRAVITY

This is a side view of a flat airplane with an upturned trailing edge. The airflow goes over the plane until it is reflected by the trailing edge. The air reflecting off the edge is the action. The reaction is the tail of the plane being pushed in the opposite direction of the reflecting air: down. That means the nose is now pointing up, and that makes the plane climb.

Similarly, imagine that the drawing is a top view of a very thin aircraft. The plane would turn right because of the reflected air pushing the tail of the plane to the left.

Let's talk some "Lite" physics, all the ideas of regular physics with a lot less numbers. One measurable parameter that sets paper airplane aerodynamics apart from full-size aircraft is a little beast called a Reynolds number.

Reynolds numbers describe one of many important aspects of airflow around any given wing. In practice, they give physicists a way to translate small-scale wind tunnel results to full-scale aircraft behavior. This is necessary because air will move differently around a small wing than a large one.

SOME EXAMPLES OF REYNOLDS NUMBERS

RN for a dust spec . . . . *1 to 10*
RN for insects . . . . *100 to 10,000*
RN for paper airplanes . . . . *20,000 to 80,000*
RN for jets . . . . *10,000,000 to 100,000,000*

In more tangible terms, a person swimming through honey would have the same Reynolds number as a honey bee flying through the air. The air seems thicker and more gooey to a bee. The air is also less willing to follow the shape of the small wing.

At very small Reynolds numbers, special steps are needed to make the airflow stick to a wing. In fact, insects like bees have veins on their wings that act as turbulators, adding turbulence to the air as it flows around the wing. This helps the airflow stick closer to the wing.

One way to add turbulence (with a minimum of drag) to a paper airplane wing is to make the leading edge as sharp as possible by creasing it well. This will have the same effect as the veins of the bee's wing, and air will follow the wing more efficiently.

Some remote control airplane builders use small strips of sandpaper for the same purpose. When placed on the leading edge of the wing, they add turbulence and increase performance.

You'll notice a difference in flight speeds for the airplanes in this book. That's caused by differences in wing loading, the specific amount of weight a standard size area of the wing lifts in flight. Wing loading is how many pounds per square foot, or grams per square inch, the wing is lifting. The larger the wing area for a given weight aircraft, the less wing loading, and the slower it will glide.

Since all the planes in this book, with the exception of the biplane, weigh exactly the same, you'll find that the smaller the wing, the faster the flight.

Now you know enough about paper airplanes to pretend that it's a science when strafing runs go awry.

Glossary

Angle of Attack: The amount an airplane's wings are slanted against the airflow.

Aspect Ratio: A mathematical way to describe the shape of a wing; the distance from wing tip to wing tip divided by the average width, or chord, of the wing. Sail planes have a high aspect ratio; an F-15 has a low aspect ratio.

Attitude: How a plane is pointed relative to its flight path or generally to the ground. Nose up, nose down, level, etc.

Bank: Raising the outside wing during a turn.

Center of Gravity: The balance point of a plane, the point through which gravity appears to act.

Center of Lift: The point at which lift seems to be acting when the plane is flying.

Control Surfaces: Surfaces that can be bent or moved to alter airflow and hence the attitude of the plane. In this book, primarily the elevators and rudders of the planes.

Crease: The result of a fold.

Dihedral Angle: The amount the wings are slanted above the horizontal. It helps to stabilize an airplane.

Drag: The resistance air exerts on a body moving through it.

Elevator: A horizontal control surface at the trailing edge of the plane (or horizontal stabilizer) that can be bent up or down to control or cause climbing or diving.

Fuselage: The body of the airplane.

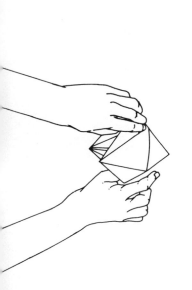

Glider: A heavier than air, engineless aircraft that flies by gliding, like a paper airplane.

Leading Edge: The forward edge of a lifting or stabilizing surface.

Lift: The amount of force acting upward against an airplane.

Maneuver: Execution of a flight pattern other than straight line, level flight; turning, diving, or climbing.

Pitch: To nose up or down.

RAT (Right About There) Fold: Inaccurate or unreferenced folding which causes irreproducible results.

Roll: To rotate the plane about the longitudinal axis.

Reynolds Number: Numerical values scientists use to discuss airflow around wings. The number is derived from the ratio of inertia or kinetic forces to viscous forces in a given fluid.

Rudder: A vertical control surface at the trailing edge of the plane (or vertical stabilizer) that can be moved to initiate or control yawing.

Trailing edge: The rear edge of a wing or stabilizer.

Trim: To make minor adjustments to the control surfaces of the plane to affect the attitude.

Winglet: A vertical stabilizer at a wing tip that adds directional stability. Usually there are two winglets on planes that use them, one on each wing.

Yaw: To turn right or left.

Symbols

Valley fold

– – – – –

Mountain fold

– · – · · – · · –

Existing crease

_____

X-ray view or guidelines

· · · · · · · · · · · · · · ·

Fold in the direction of arrow

Fold behind

Unfold

Fold and unfold

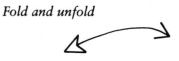

Push in, sink, squash, or reverse

⇨

Turn model over

Watch this point

o

DARTS

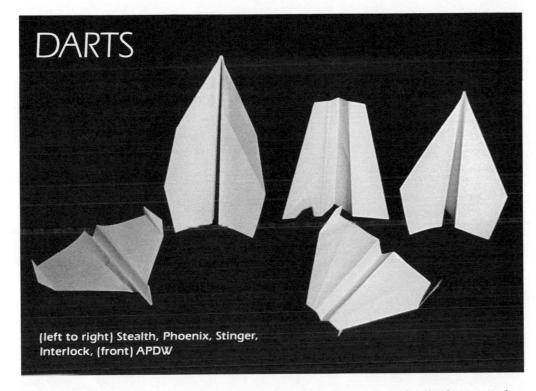

(left to right) Stealth, Phoenix, Stinger, Interlock, (front) APDW

These are muscle planes. The Stinger and Interlock are specifically fine assault planes that hold up under repeated high-speed impacts. They all travel great distances but, with the exception of the Phoenix, they do not ride the thermals or glide for minutes at a time. Darts fly very well outdoors in high wind because of their durability. My testing space is a 60-foot long studio; in order for a dart to be considered a success, it had to fly level across this space and hit the opposite wall with a resounding smack. These planes passed the test.

The Phoenix

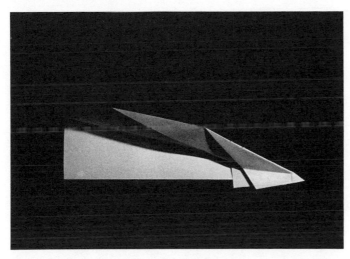

The Phoenix is a great multi-purpose aircraft and will handle a fast or slow toss. It has good speed, distance, and accuracy. The Phoenix flies indoors or out and it's very easy to fold.

STEP 1 ▼

Fold and unfold diagonals, and then
flip the page over.

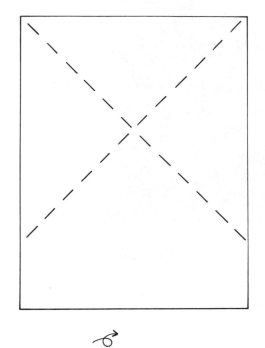

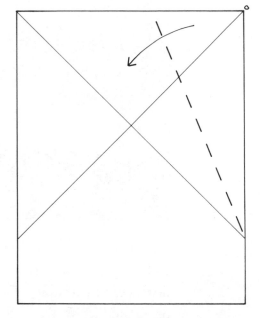

STEP 2 ▲

Fold the marked corner to the diagonal
crease and line up the edge of the paper
with the crease.

STEP 3 ▼

Make the same fold as in Step 2 for the left side. Use the end of the marked crease as a guide for positioning the marked corner.

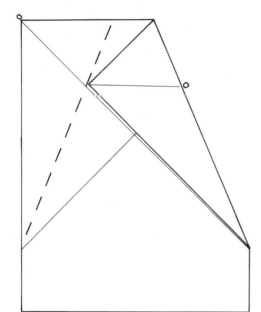

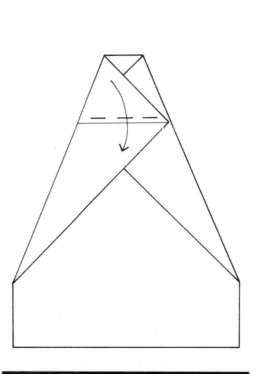

STEP 4 ▲

Fold the top down by following the existing crease.

STEP 5 ▼

Fold the plane in half leaving all the
layers exposed.

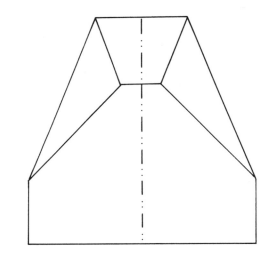

STEP 6 ▲

Fold the marked corner to the base
shown with a mark. The diagram shows
the crease starting exactly in the corner
of the nose. It's good to give this crease
a little breathing room, particularly on
thick sheets of paper.

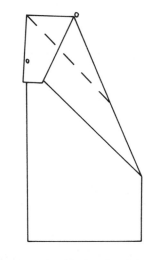

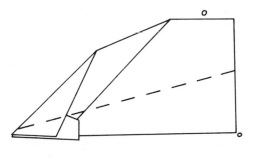

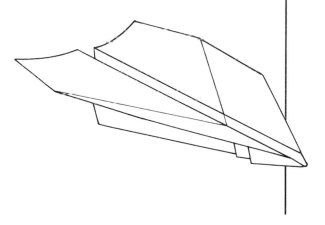

This is the "Phoenix Fold" for the wing. Make a crease that starts just above the corner of the nose. Fold the wing down so that the marked edge just touches the marked corner. Do not line up any edges of the wing directly with the fuselage. The resulting crease should have a gentle slope from just above the nose to the tail of the airplane. The marked corner of the fuselage should just barely be visible.

Set dihedral angle and sharpen the leading edges of the wings. Trim as needed. As with most planes, add a little up elevator for faster tosses or outdoor flight. Dihedral, or wing angle, can vary from almost flat to severely "V" shaped. This tolerance helps keep it flying in a wide range of conditions. The Phoenix has good accuracy, good distance, and is a good dart-like glider.

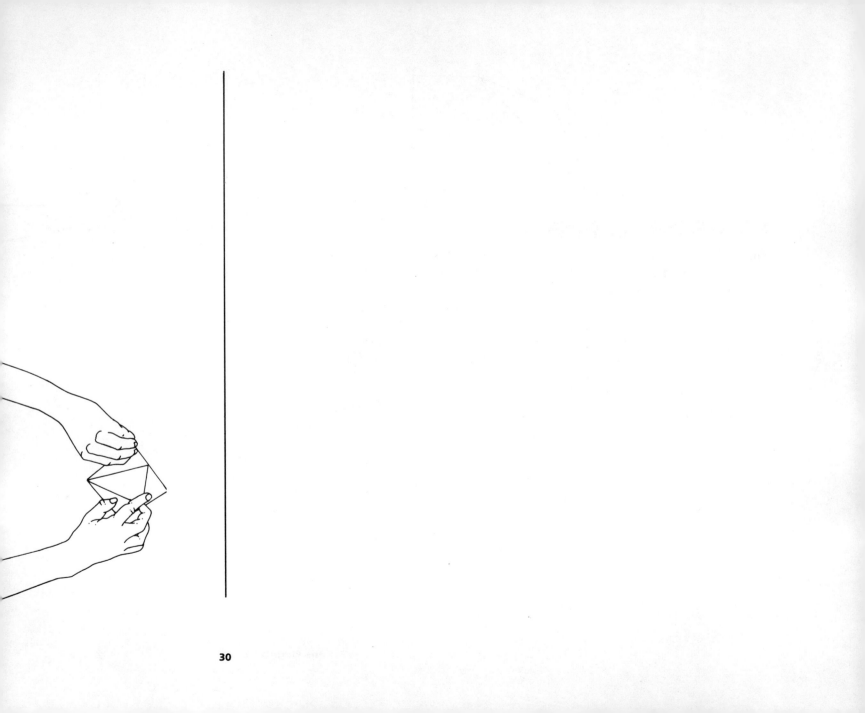

30

APDW (All Purpose Delta Wing)

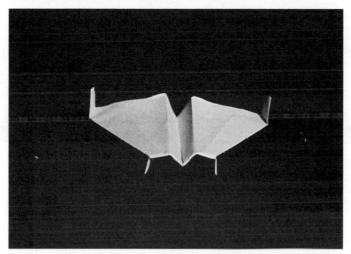

The APDW is a fast dart with landing gear. It will often bounce off a smooth surface when landing. The first step is a waterbomb base which is demonstrated in the flip-through animation. Indoor or outdoor thrills are available.

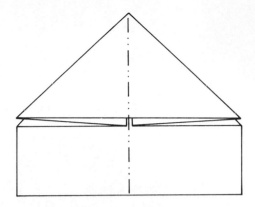

STEP 1 ▶

Start with a waterbomb base. Fold the base in half. The flip-through animation shows the construction of a waterbomb base.

STEP 2 ▼

Pull the outside flaps down.

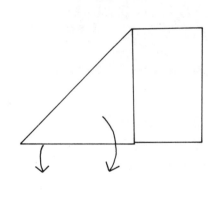

STEP 3 ▼

Fold top diagonal edge to the fuselage and unfold.

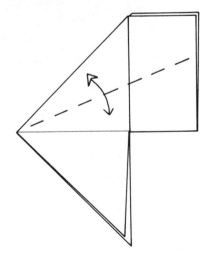

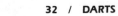

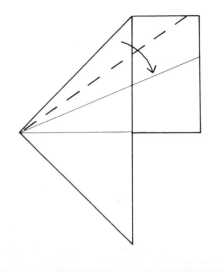

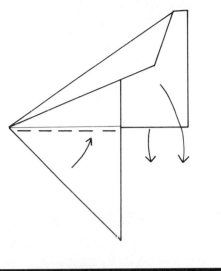

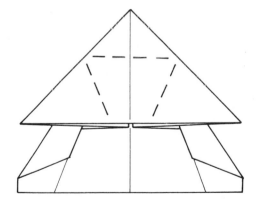

STEP 4 ▲

Fold the top diagonal edge to the crease created in step 3.

STEP 5 ▲

Pull the triangular flaps back up and open up the fold from step 1.

STEP 6 ◀

Fold the outside corners in like an origami paper cup. For reference points, unfold entire plane and fold as in steps 2 and 3 of the Phoenix.

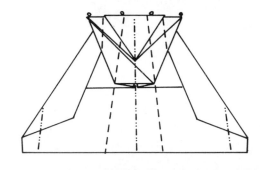

STEP 7 ▲

This is a synopsis of the wing, landing gear and winglet folds. It may be helpful to remake the fuselage crease, make the wing folds, and then return your plane to this position to study the landing gear folds. RAT fold the wings and then make the winglets and landing gear parallel. Proper landing gear folds call for the points marked to be folded to the wing folds.

Set the dihedral angle and trim as needed. The APDW (All Purpose Delta Wing) has good indoor distance and is also a fun outdoor stunt plane. Keep the leading edges sharp; it will probably need some up elevator. Truly all-purpose.

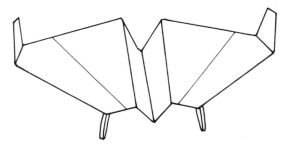

Interlock

This thing is a rocket and may be the fastest plane I've ever built. The Interlock has one of the heaviest wing loading designs in the book. If you're a beginning folder, there will be some new moves here for you. The waterbomb base, sink fold, and squash fold are all in the flip-through animations, so don't worry. Test this one anywhere there is plenty of room, in high wind or dead calm. You'll be amazed.

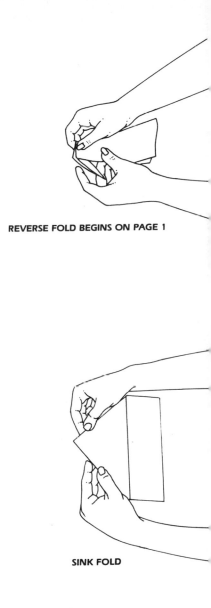

REVERSE FOLD BEGINS ON PAGE 1

SINK FOLD

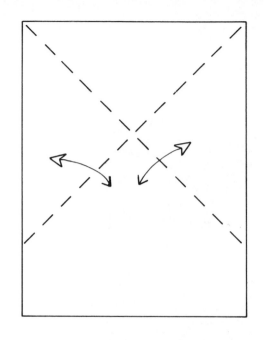

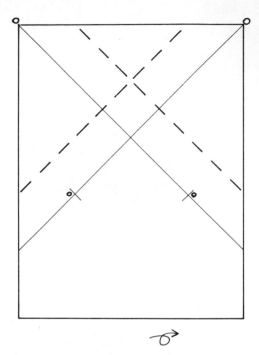

STEP 1 ▲

Make diagonal creases and unfold.

STEP 2 ▲

Locate the halfway point on the lower legs of the diagonals by placing the end of the crease on the point where the creases cross. Make a pinch mark only. Fold the upper corners to the pinch marks and unfold. Flip over.

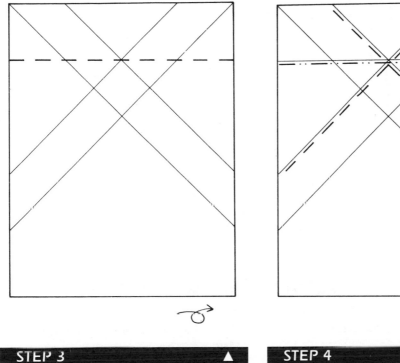

STEP 3 ▲

Valley fold across the intersection of the new diagonals. Flip over.

STEP 4 ▲

Waterbomb the upper diagonals. A waterbomb base is shown in the flip-through animation.

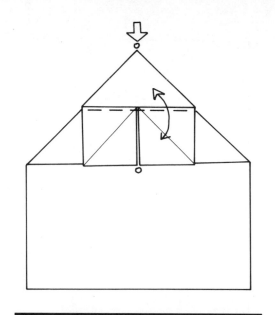

STEP 5 ▲

Sink the triangle. A sink fold is shown in the flip-through animation.

STEP 6 ▲

Squash fold where shown. A squash fold is shown in the flip-through animation.

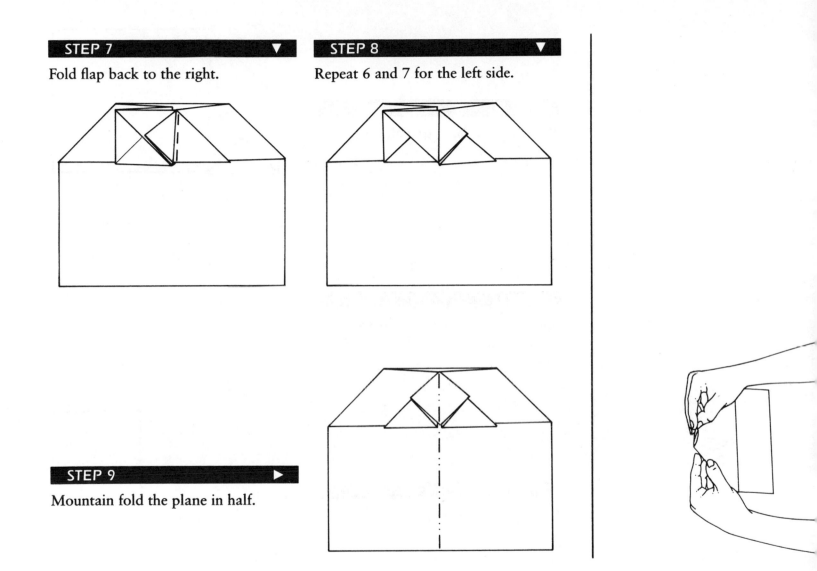

STEP 7 ▼

Fold flap back to the right.

STEP 8 ▼

Repeat 6 and 7 for the left side.

STEP 9 ▶

Mountain fold the plane in half.

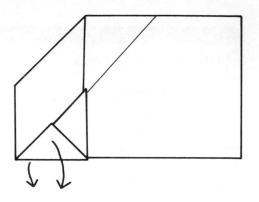

STEP 10 ▶

Pull down the small triangle on each side.

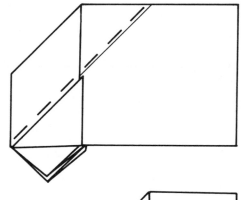

STEP 11 ▶

Fold along the existing crease to make the front edge meet the fuselage. Repeat on the other side.

STEP 12 ▶

Tuck the triangle into the pocket.

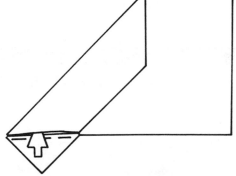

STEP 13 ▶

Make a Phoenix type of wing fold—the marked edge meets the corner.

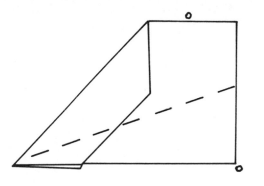

Adjust for symmetry and give the wings a slight upward curve. Trim as needed. Using the main wing crease, you can vary the wing angle almost as much as the Phoenix. Increase the wing curvature by bending slightly up about a quarter inch from where it connects to the fuselage. This completes the dihedral adjustment. It may also need just a touch of up elevator. There's no problem getting the Interlock across a regular size living room or most lecture halls. This plane can be appreciated in either a large indoor space or outdoors. Trim for giant loops or fly in high wind situations.

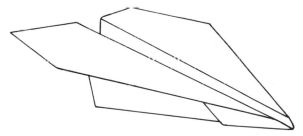

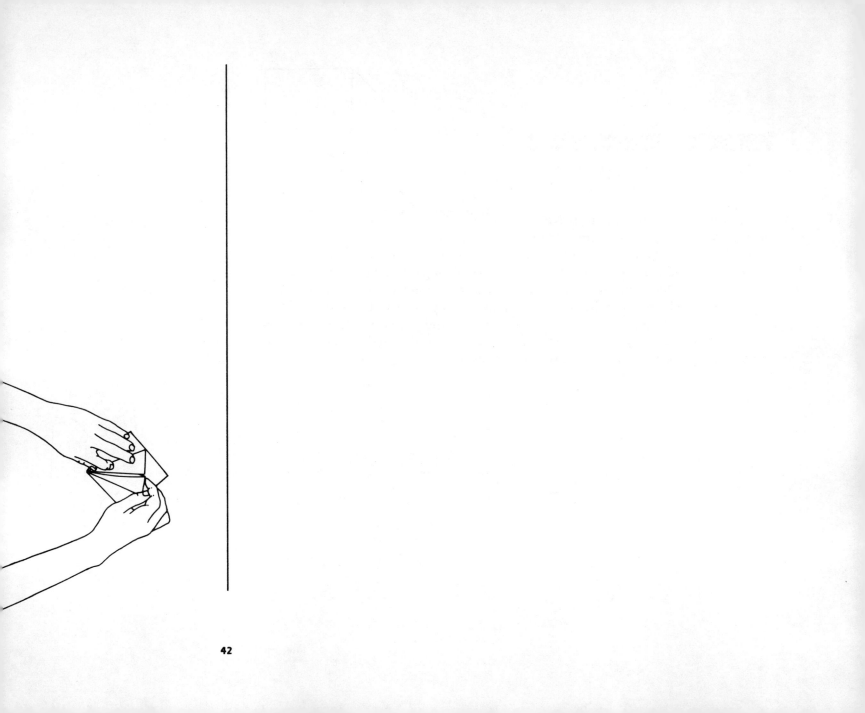

Stealth

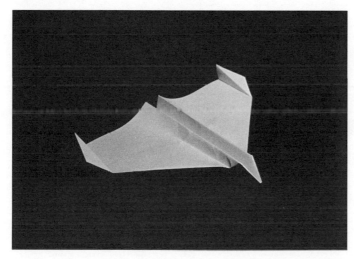

The Stealth is a great distance model indoors and a fun stunt plane outdoors. It's simple to fold and easy to trim. Sharp creasing is the key to this very fast, very fun, sharp-looking plane.

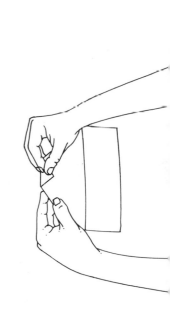

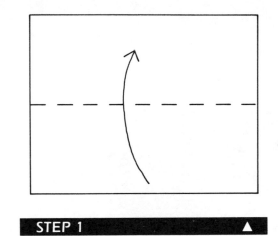

STEP 1 ▲

Fold in half.

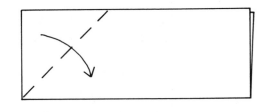

STEP 2 ▲

Fold the corners to the center crease.

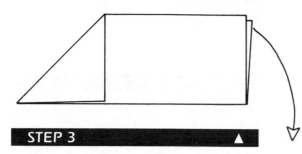

Unfold the center crease.

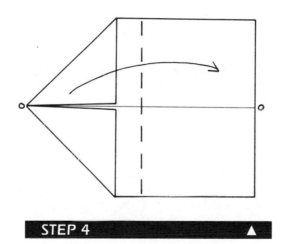

Fold the model in half by folding the
point to the end of the center crease.

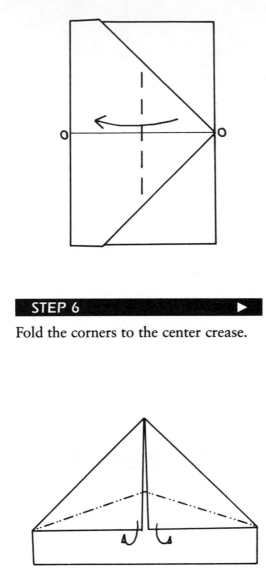

STEP 5 ◀

Fold the point back to the creased edge from step 4.

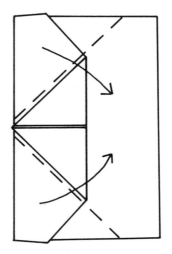

STEP 6 ▶

Fold the corners to the center crease.

STEP 7 ◀

Using the creased edge you made in step 5 as a guide, fold the flaps under that creased edge.

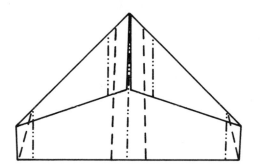

STEP 8 ◀

Fold the plane in half along the center crease. Make a RAT fold for the main wing fold, parallel with the fuselage fold. Make the winglets by RAT folding parallel to the wing fold, then diagonally across the flap you created with the RAT fold. Finally, make two creases that start at the nose at about half the width of the fuselage from the wing fold. Fold from the nose to the end of the layering. This partial crease should be parallel to the wing fold.

STEP 9 ▶

Add some up elevator and set dihedral or wing angle, checking the wing curvatures with the photo.

The Stealth's high wing loading makes it a high speed wonder. Make sure the curvature of the trailing edges match. You will need to trim in some up elevator and make the partial wing creases very sharp to help set the wing curvature. Bend the leading edge of the wing up slightly where it meets these creases if the airplane noses down after dramatic trimming. The Stealth is so fast, most people never see it coming.

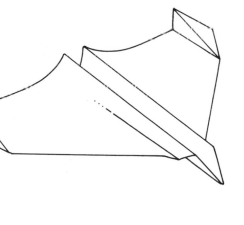

Stinger

The Stinger is a pocket rocket named for the Stinger missile. It's perfect for high speed strafing runs or bullet-like attacks. It offers a new base fold with which you can experiment. Fly the Stinger indoors or out.

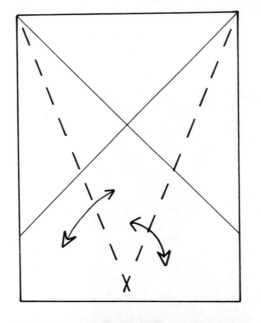

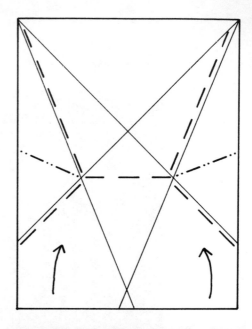

Make diagonal creases. Then fold lower corners to the diagonals.

Valley fold along existing creases while making some new ones. The idea is to create a waterbomb-like base as shown in the next step (rotated). A waterbomb base is shown in the flip-through animation.

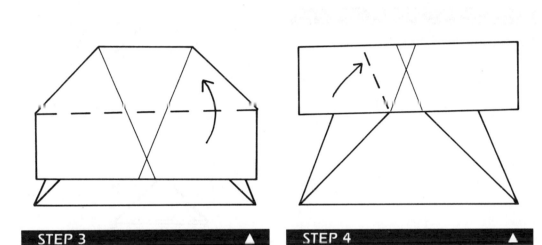

Rotate model ½ turn from step 2. Valley fold the flap up at the corners.

Valley fold the flap as far as you can.

WATERBOMB BASE BEGINS ON PAGE 146

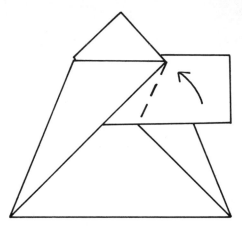

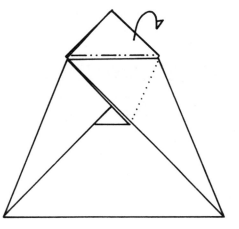

STEP 5 ▶

Repeat for the right side.

STEP 6 ▶

Mountain fold all flaps back and tuck into the far pocket.

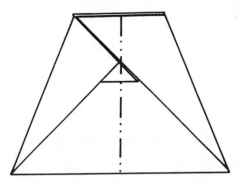

STEP 7 ◀

Mountain fold in half.

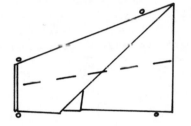

STEP 8 ▶

Make the wing folds by folding the top edge to the fuselage fold.

Adjust dihedral, or wing angle, and trim as needed. It usually needs a bit of up elevator and a slight dihedral angle. The Stinger is very fast and accurate.

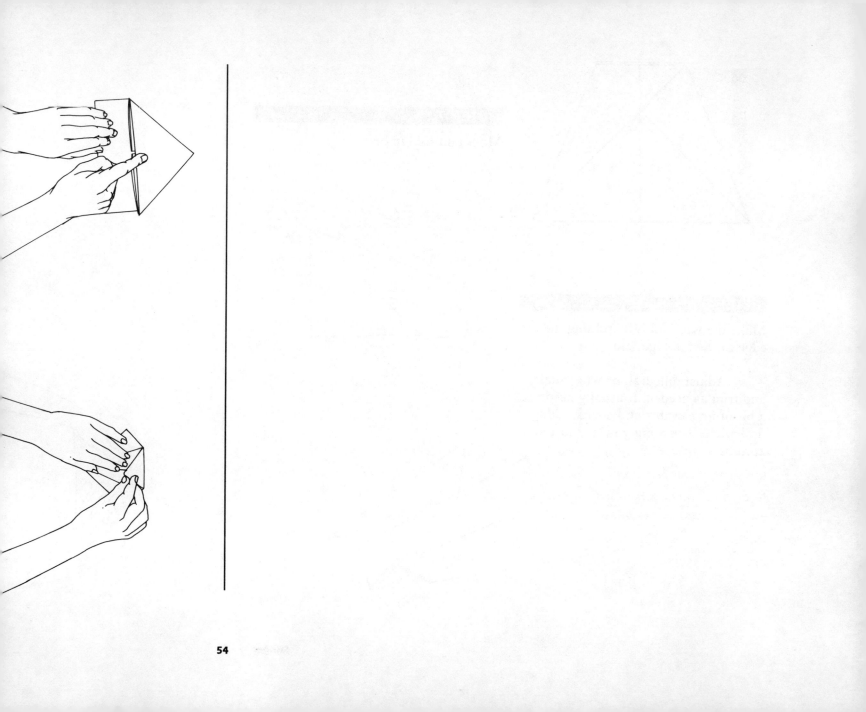

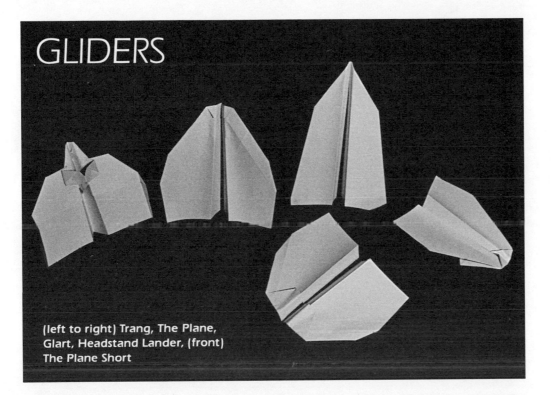

GLIDERS

(left to right) Trang, The Plane,
Glart, Headstand Lander, (front)
The Plane Short

Time aloft was the goal for this group of aircraft and, like the Darts, they had to span the 60-foot distance mark to be part of the team. These planes also had to demonstrate exceptional soaring capability. In testing, I had to park them repeatedly on my neighbor's rooftop, about 150 feet away from where I launched them. These gliders can handle a hard throw and level out into a nice glide. They are the best from a technical point of view—glide ratio, time aloft, and stall recovery. Each has earned its way into this chapter.

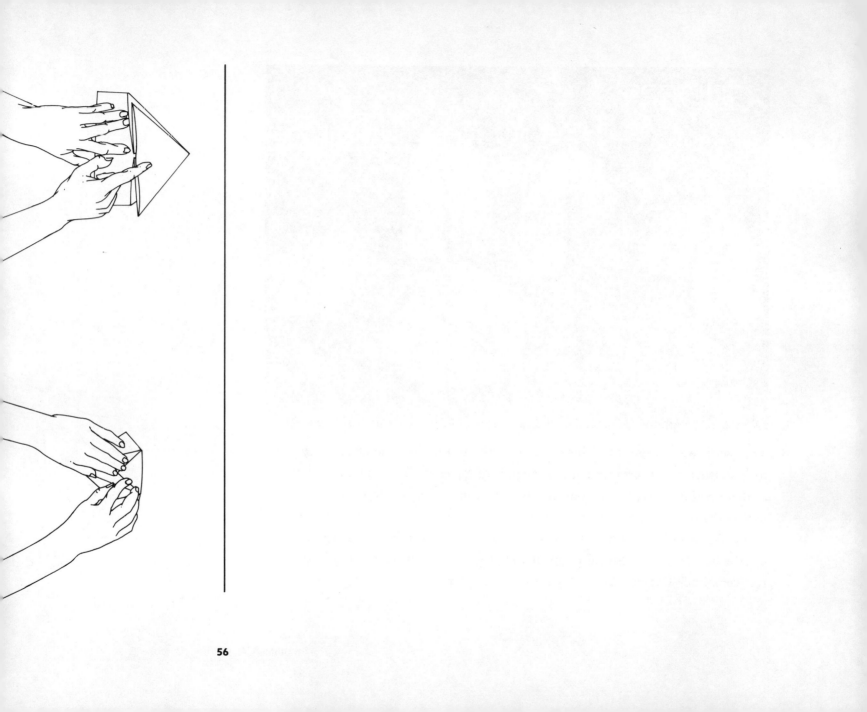

The Plane

This is simply the best plane I've invented to date. If you take the time to trim the Plane correctly, you won't believe the flights. It's easy to fold and fantastic to fly.

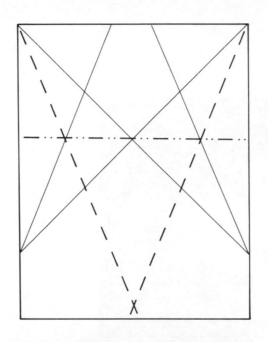

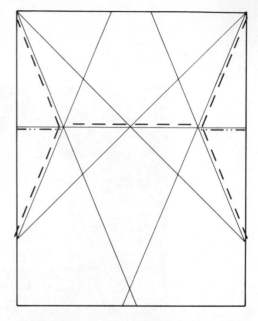

STEP 1　　　　　　　▲

Fold like the Phoenix to step 3 and unfold. Make similar folds for the lower
corners. Then make a mountain fold
across the intersection of the diagonal
creases.

STEP 2　　　　　　　▲

Fold along existing creases to create
a waterbomb-like base. A waterbomb
base is demonstrated in the flip-through
animation.

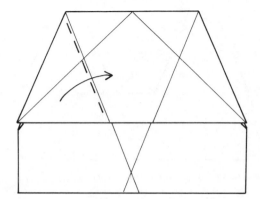

Valley fold existing crease.

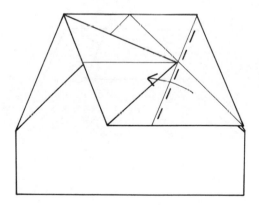

STEP 4   ◀

Repeat for the right side.

STEP 5 ▶

Valley fold the section along the existing crease.

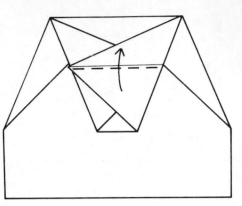

STEP 6 ▶

Mountain fold the flap back.

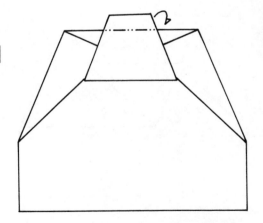

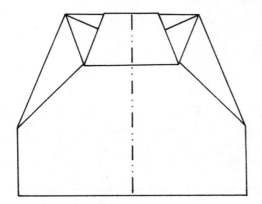

STEP 7 ◄

Mountain fold the plane in half.

STEP 8 ►

Make a valley fold after tucking the corner into the slot shown by the arrow.

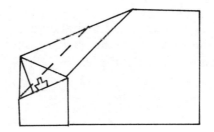

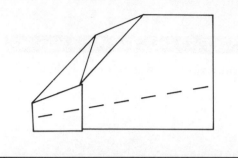

Make the wing fold so that you fold approximately in half the thickest section shown (the quadrilateral shape).

Adjust dihedral or wing angle, and set a gentle bend in the wing surface where shown in the group photo. Trim as needed. The plane is a great indoor/ outdoor glider. Proper trimming can be tricky. When adding dihedral angle, bend the wing where shown in the photo. Most aircraft with stiff leading edges can benefit from this technique. By bending the wing instead of adjusting the main wing crease, you can preserve the strength of the crease. This is important for faster-flying aircraft.

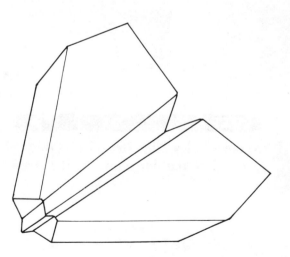

The Plane Short

The Plane Short is a combination of the Phoenix and the Plane. It's easier to trim than the Plane, but has a slightly lower glide ratio. The Plane Short will fly anywhere and usually out-fly the competition.

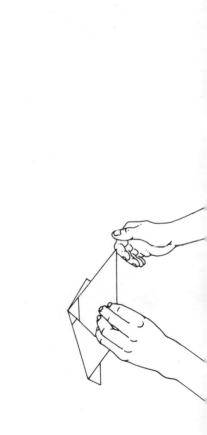

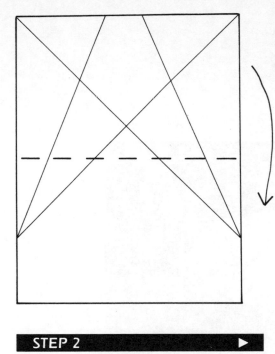

STEP 1 ◀

Fold like the Phoenix to step 3 and unfold. Then fold in half.

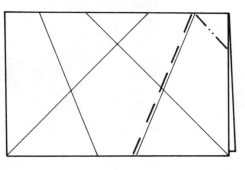

STEP 2 ▶

Fold along the existing crease and force a new crease to happen—the one marked with a mountain fold.

STEP 3 ▶

Repeat for the left side.

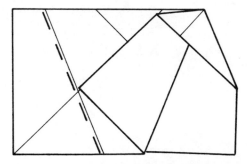

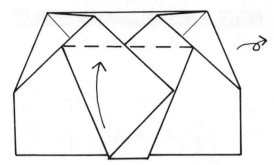

Fold this section up as far as you can without straining the pockets created from steps 2 and 3. Flip over.

Valley fold top to almost meet the main folded edge. Leave a little breathing room.

Valley fold the whole flap over along the main creased edge.

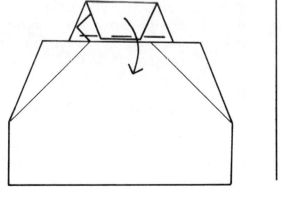

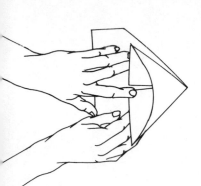

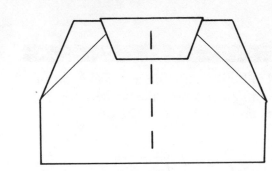

Valley fold the plane in half.

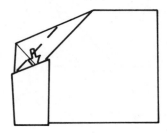

Make a valley fold after tucking the corner into the slot shown by the arrow.

Make the wing fold (it's a RAT), a gently sloping crease leaving plenty of fuselage to hang on to.

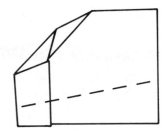

Adjust the dihedral or wing angle so that it matches the photo. Set a gentle bend in the wing surface where shown in the photo, using the same technique as the Plane, and trim as needed. The Plane Short is another great glider. It's a bit easier to trim than the full-size version. The fuselage should be slightly taller than the Plane's. It flies a little faster than the Plane, but the glide ratio isn't quite as high. The Plane Short will fly in a wide variety of wind situations.

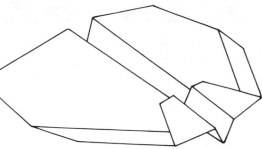

Glart

Is it a glider or a dart? You decide. The Glart delivers a better than average performance in either category. It's an easy-to-fold, high-performance plane that works well indoors or out.

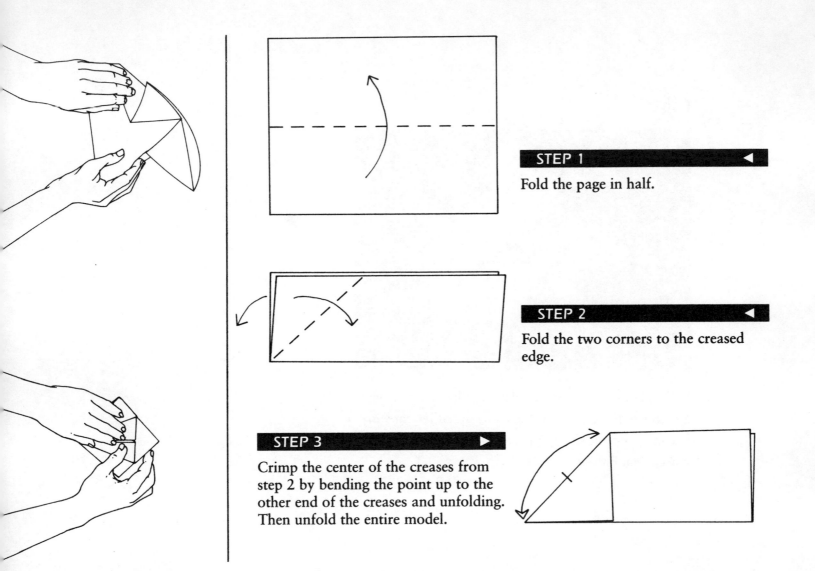

STEP 1 ◀

Fold the page in half.

STEP 2 ◀

Fold the two corners to the creased edge.

STEP 3 ▶

Crimp the center of the creases from step 2 by bending the point up to the other end of the creases and unfolding. Then unfold the entire model.

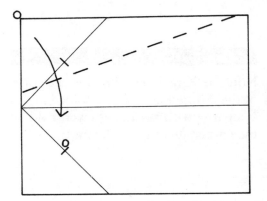

STEP 4

Fold one corner to the crimp mark on the opposite side of the center crease.

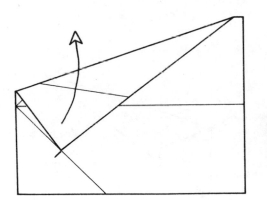

STEP 5

Unfold and repeat for the other side. Then refold both flaps as in step 6.

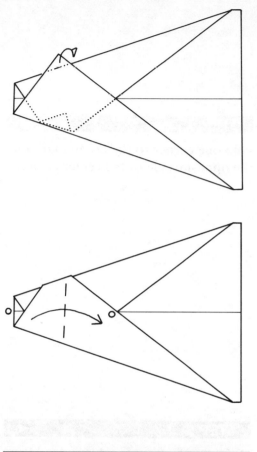

Note the X-ray view showing the corner of the covered layer being folded in sympathy with the upper layer. Fold the corner sticking out behind.

Fold the small raw edge to the point where the layers cross.

Mountain fold the plane in half along the existing crease.

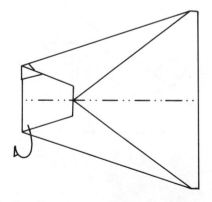

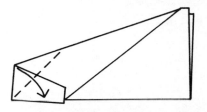 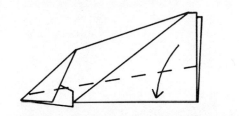

Fold the front edge to the main fuselage fold.

RAT fold the wings from close to the nose sloping up toward the tail. The wings extend well past the fuselage when you're making the crease.

Set a slight wing or dihedral angle and trim as needed. Is it a glider or is it a dart?

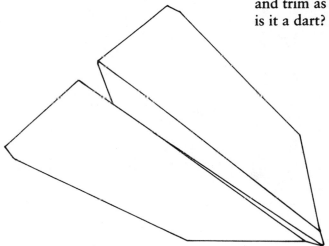

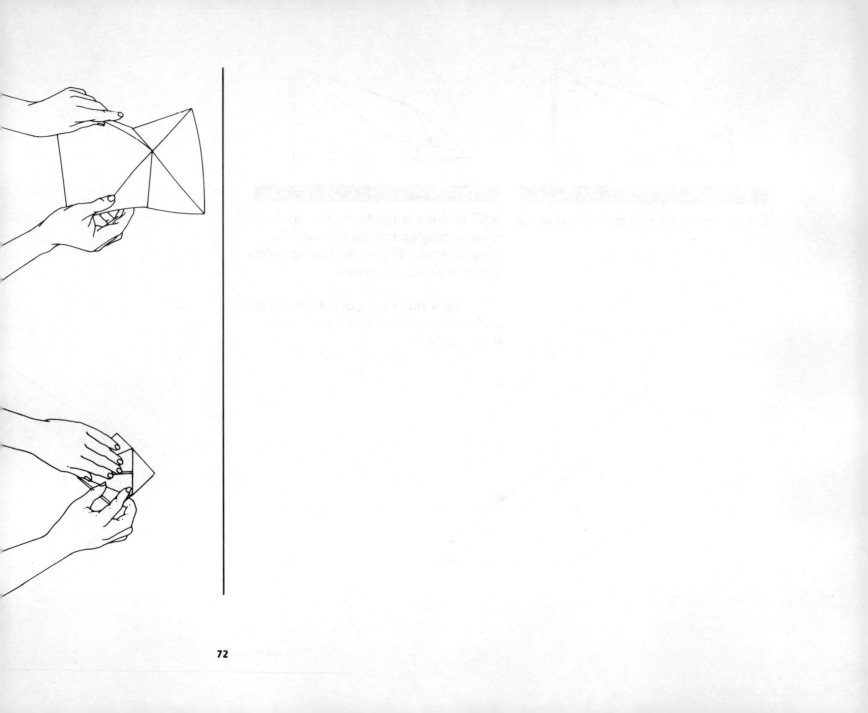

Trang

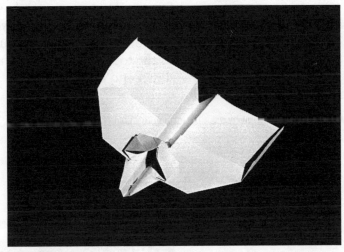

The Trang is a good indoor/outdoor plane, and a great-looking glider that will give you distance and time aloft. Patience is required for folding this one.

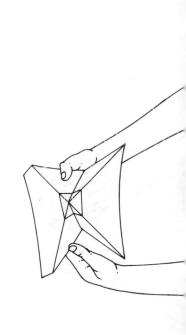

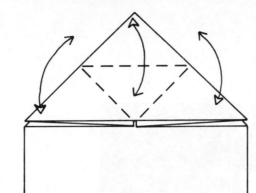

STEP 1 ◄

Start with a waterbomb base. The flip-through animation shows you how. Fold and unfold the two outside points to the top. Then fold the top straight down and unfold.

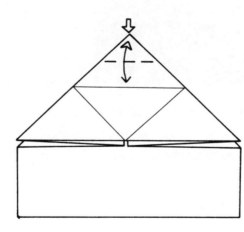

STEP 2 ◄

Fold the top triangle in half and unfold. Then sink the triangle.

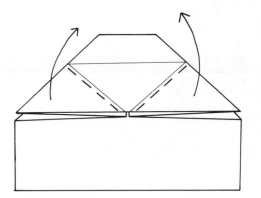

Fold up the two points.

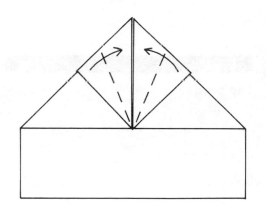

Fold the edge of the flaps to the center.

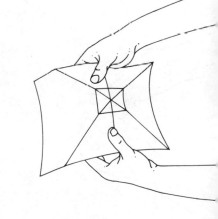

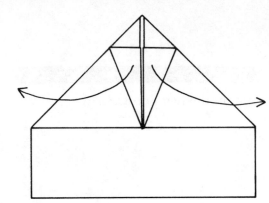

Unfold flaps.

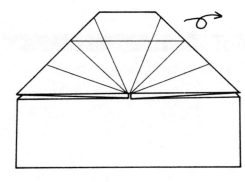

Flip over.

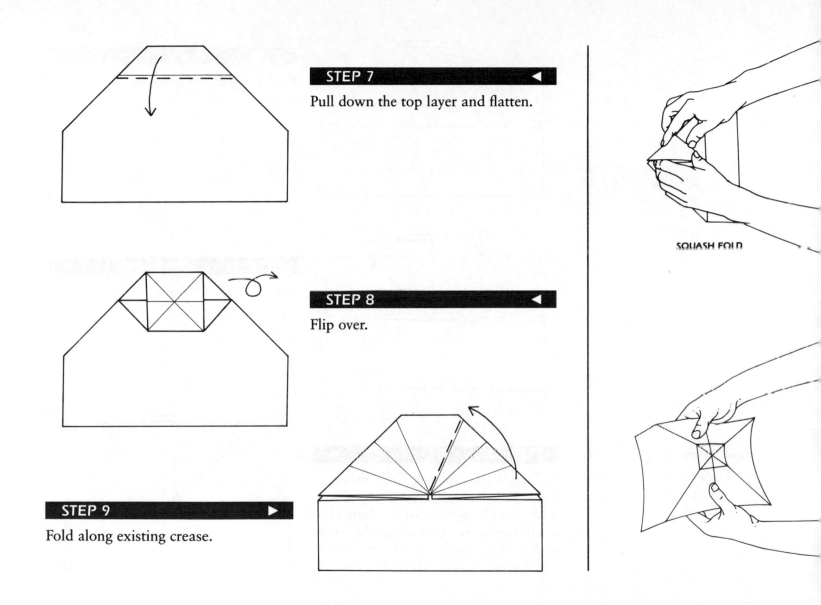

Pull down the top layer and flatten.

SQUASH FOLD

Flip over.

Fold along existing crease.

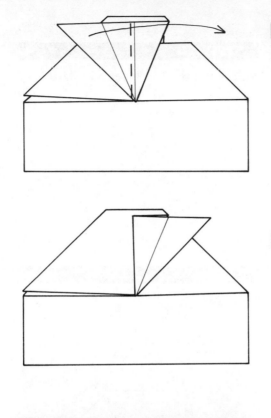

STEP 10 ◄

Fold along existing crease.

STEP 11 ◄

Repeat 9 and 10 for the left side.

STEP 12 ►

Pull down the top layer while valley folding the bottom layer (X-ray valley fold). Also keep track of the dotted line; it will turn into a mountain fold for the middle layer. Study the resulting drawing in step 13. This is a tricky step.

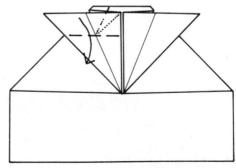

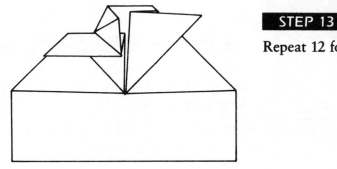

Repeat 12 for the right side.

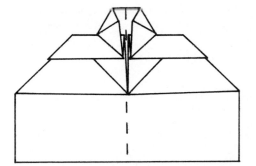

STEP 14 ◀

Valley fold the plane in half.

STEP 15 ▶

Make the wing folds by starting at the nose, just under the top corner. Slope the crease gently up to the rear of the plane. Make the winglets parallel.

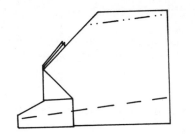

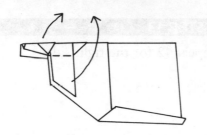

STEP 16 ◄

Fold up the flaps parallel with the wing folds and slip one inside the other. See step 17 specifics.

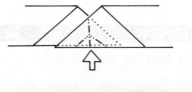

STEP 17 ▲

This close-up drawing shows how to interlock the flaps. Mountain fold the center and then reverse fold a notch in the rear to match the notch left in front. A reverse fold is shown in the flip-through animation.

Setting the dihedral or wing angle will open up the triangle nicely. This airplane is less likely to flop open in flight, so it won't need as much dihedral angle as some other aircraft. Trim as needed.

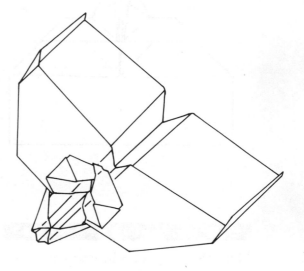

Headstand Lander

The Headstand Lander is a good glider and when properly made, this plane will glide to a skidding landing and rest on its nose and landing gear, the resting position for which it was named. It's a good indoor/outdoor aircraft that can be tricky to fold.

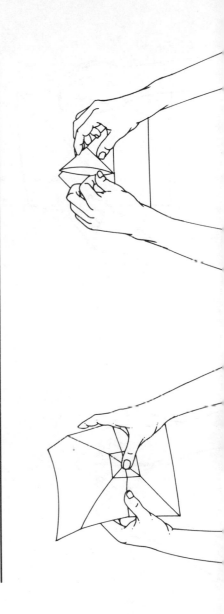

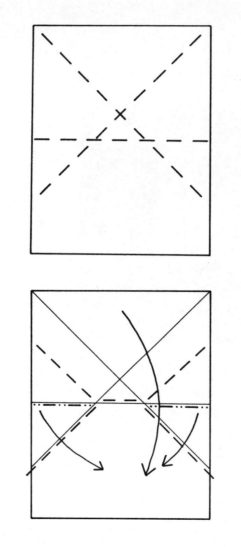

Make diagonal folds and unfold. Fold in half and unfold.

Following the center crease and the lower legs of the diagonal creases, make a waterbomb-like base by pressing the model together and creating two new creases where shown. A waterbomb base is shown in the flip-through animation.

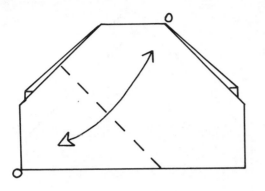

STEP 3 ◀

Fold the lower left corner up to meet the upper right corner. Repeat for the lower right corner.

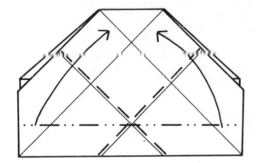

STEP 4 ◀

Make a mountain fold across the intersection of the creases from step 3 and parallel to the raw edge. Then waterbomb using the creases from steps 3 and 4.

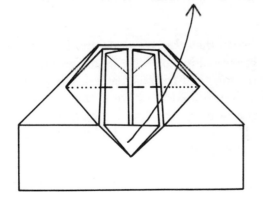

STEP 5 ◀

Fold the waterbombed point up. Let the two corners be your limiting points so that the crease ends up where shown with the valley fold and X-ray lines.

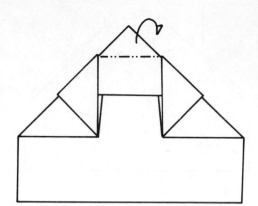

STEP 6 ▶

Fold the top point back.

STEP 7 ▶

Make the wing and fuselage folds. Make the landing gear folds by starting at the corner of the triangle and ending at the center of the other side.

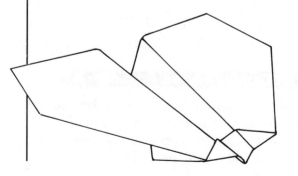

Set the dihedral angle and landing gear position by looking at the illustration, and trim as needed. Give it a slight dihedral or wing angle using the same method as the Plane. The Headstand Lander offers versatile, indoor/outdoor fun.

SPECIALTY INDOOR/OUTDOOR

(left to right) Starship Shuttle, Wind Devil, Interlock Biplane, Starfighter, AWACS, (front) Tube

Designing a plane usually begins with a general design goal. The goal can be anything: a tunnel fuselage, a two-piece construction, auxiliary wings, landing gear, or a specific flight pattern. The planes in this section are special because they met their design goals in unique and efficient ways. They have met the 60-foot distance requirement. They fly well indoors and handle most outdoor wind conditions very well. Specialty planes are the most demanding to build. Enter this arena with patience and you'll be rewarded with outstanding paper airplanes.

ZARAGOZA 27 de Diciembre de 1988

Querido amigo:

Te agradecemos sinceramente tu participación en el 2º Certamen Internacional de Aviones de Papel (2ⁿᵈ Contest International of Origami Paperplanes).

Las marcas que consiguieron tus aviones en los dos lanzamientos que se efectuaron en el certamen son:

Avión	Distancia (m)		Tiempo (s)	
	1º	2º	1º	2º
Interlock Biplane	3,50	5,10	4,89"	3,78"
Interlock	14,20	16,60	2,05"	2,90"
Plane short	16,10	9,05	2,36"	6,50"
The Plane	10,60	5,90	1,85"	1,03"
Star Fighter	--	**29,10**	3,37"	6,37"
Swan	6,70	7,20	2,10"	2,39"

Donde tu avión **Star Fighter**, con la marca del segundo lanzamiento logró el <u>primer puesto</u> en la <u>modalidad de distancia</u>.

Asimismo te enviamos la fotografía del instante del lanzamiento de cada uno de tus aviones.

Esperamos tu participación en el próximo concurso, sobre el cual te enviaremos cumplida noticia en su momento, afectuosamente,

Juan Bautista Arroyo
Secretario del
Grupo Zaragozano de Papiroflexia.

Starfighter

The Starfighter won the distance category in the Second International Origami Paper Airplane Competition in Zaragoza, Spain. It's also been flown upside down (tunnel on the bottom) with success. You'll, be raising eyebrows from the very first toss whether indoors or out.

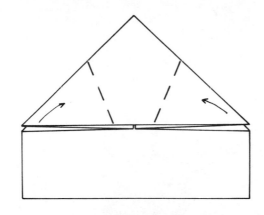

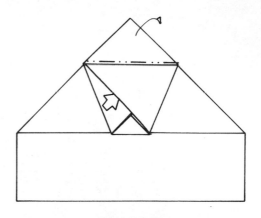

Start with a waterbomb base. The flip-through animation shows how to water-bomb. Fold the corners up as if you were making an origami paper cup. If you are unfamiliar with this idea, you can give yourself guidelines for corner placement by unfolding the waterbomb, performing steps 2 and 3 of the Phoenix, and then remaking the waterbomb.

Insert one flap inside the other and then fold the top triangle back.

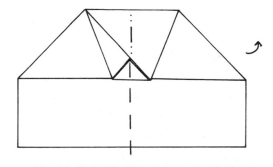

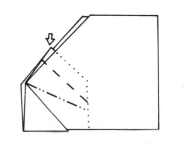

STEP 3 ▲

This is a tricky fold. Note that the interlocked flaps get mountain folded while the entire fuselage gets valley folded. This will give you a tunnel effect. Make sure the flaps stay interlocked well during this step.

STEP 4 ▲

The mountain and valley folds shown actually happen to the tunnel. Pinch the tunnel together at the top and press it down into the fuselage to complete this step. The valley fold should be parallel with the top of the tunnel and the fuselage. The illustration below shows a front view after the fold is complete.

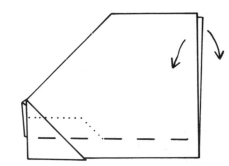

Make the main wing fold by folding down the wing even with the valley fold from step 4. The fold should be parallel with the fuselage.

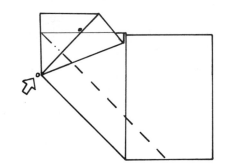

Reverse the point marked. A reverse fold is shown in the flip-through animation. This is easier if you make the valley fold shown first. The valley fold should be parallel with the diagonal edge of the wing.

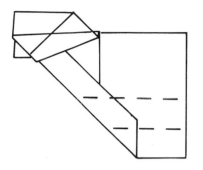

STEP 7 ◀

Make the other wing folds by folding the short edge of the wing to the main wing crease, unfolding and then folding the short edge to the new crease.

Set wing angles using the drawing and add up elevator, if needed, to the surfaces shown with the arrows. Trim as needed. It's very fast, very accurate, and exciting to fly. The complex folding is well worth the effort. Wing symmetry and sharp leading edges are the keys for great flights.

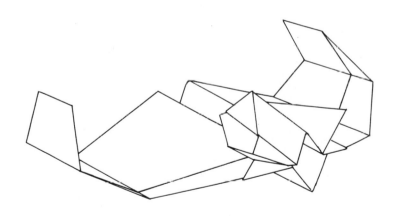

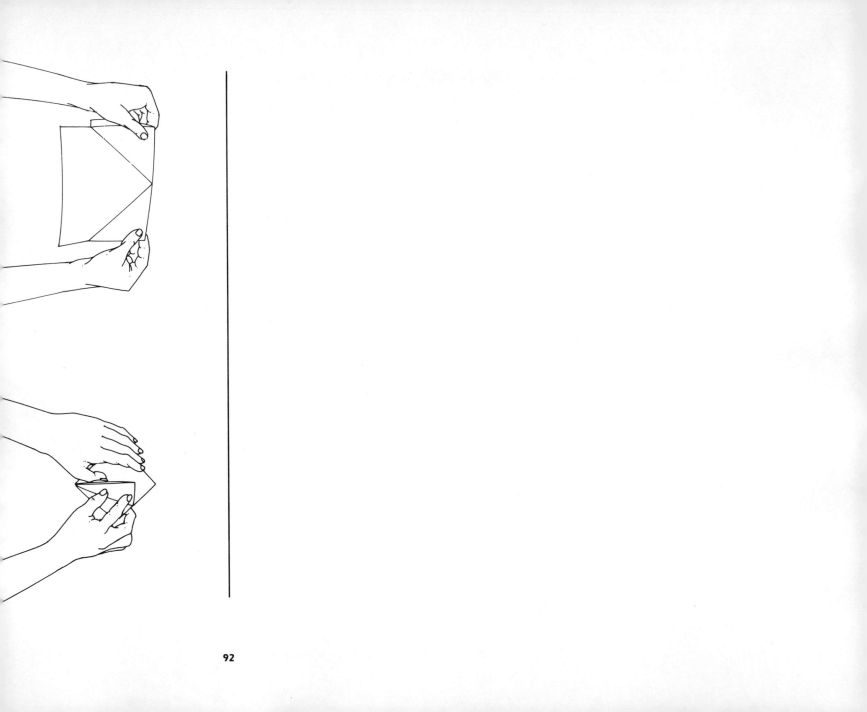

AWACS
(Airplane with Auxiliary Control Surfaces)

The AWACS starts with the same base as the Stinger, but gets more complex from there. Using more RAT folds than any plane in the book, it's the hardest plane to fold. It's an origami masterpiece and a fine aircraft indoors or out.

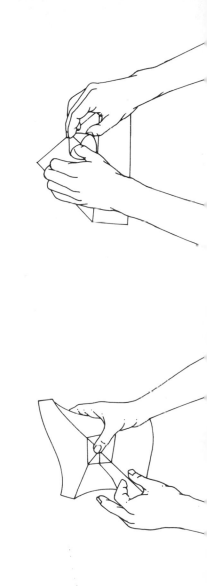

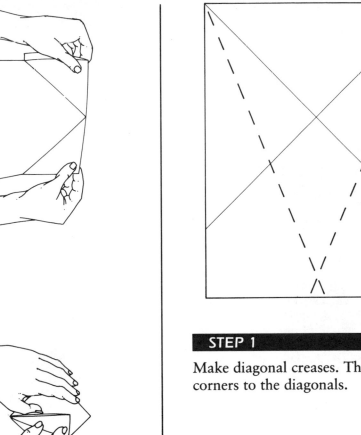

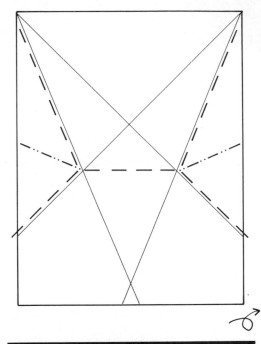

Make diagonal creases. Then fold lower corners to the diagonals.

Valley fold along existing creases while making some new ones. The idea is to create a waterbomb-like base as shown in the next step. Check the flip-through animation for waterbomb technique.

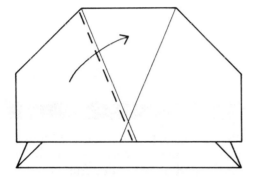

STEP 3 ▲

Valley fold the flap up at the crease (see Stinger base).

STEP 4 ▲

Valley fold the flap so that the marked corners come together and the new crease meets the intersection of creases shown in step 3. Unfold and repeat for the right side. Then assemble both creases as in step 5.

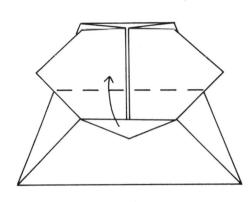

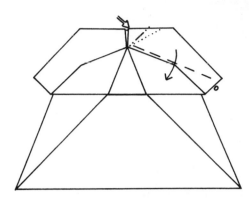

Fold the triangle up as far as possible.

Valley fold the top layer down while squash folding the corner marked. Note that the end of the valley fold should be close to the center of the edge marked. You may need to crowd the existing layers to make that happen. A squash fold is shown in the flip-through animation.

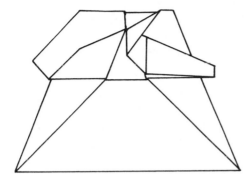

STEP 7 ▲

Repeat for the left side.

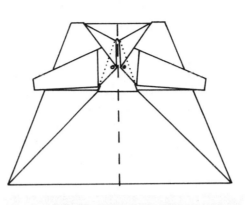

STEP 8 ▲

Tuck the marked flaps under the triangle shown with the dotted line. Then valley fold in half.

STEP 9 ▶

Make the wing folds by pulling the wing as far down in front as possible, while leaving the struts standing. Let the wing fold gently slope as it reaches the rear of the plane.

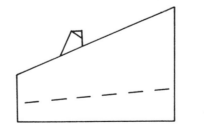

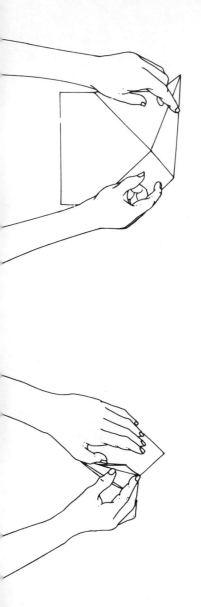

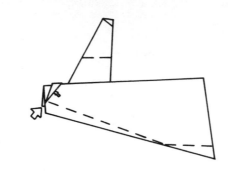

Reinforce the leading edge of the wing by valley folding a small portion so that the leading corner can be tucked under the flap shown. Make the winglet valley fold intersect the leading edge fold and be parallel to the wing fold. RAT fold the auxiliary control surfaces so that they are parallel with the wing surfaces. Reverse fold the nose.

Set dihedral or wing angle on all wing surfaces and trim as needed.

The AWACS flies surprisingly well in most outdoor situations. It will do well in all but the most windy conditions. AWACS is a must for the paper pilot looking to get recognized as a truly fine craftsman.

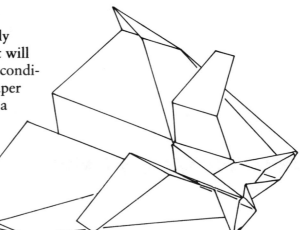

Interlock Biplane

When built with care, this sturdy aircraft will fly in all but the most windy situations. During the finishing steps you're folding a lot of layers at one time, so patience is the key. If you can fold the Interlock, you can fold the Interlock Biplane. Precision folding is a must for this unique design.

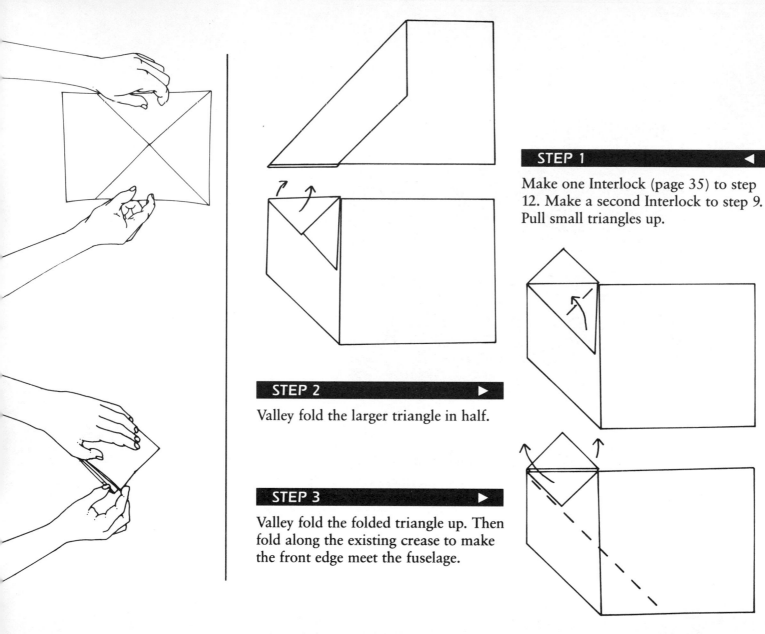

STEP 1 ◀

Make one Interlock (page 35) to step 12. Make a second Interlock to step 9. Pull small triangles up.

STEP 2 ▶

Valley fold the larger triangle in half.

STEP 3 ▶

Valley fold the folded triangle up. Then fold along the existing crease to make the front edge meet the fuselage.

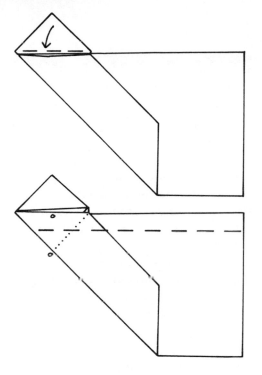

STEP 4 ◄

Tuck the outside triangle only into the pocket. Repeat for other side.

STEP 5 ◄

Make a wing fold by folding the triangle tucked inside in half, making the fold parallel to the fuselage. Unfold the wing fold.

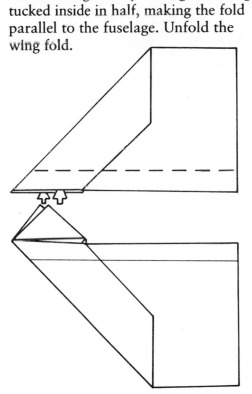

STEP 6 ▶

Insert the lower section into the upper section and then fold the wings just as before, making a fold parallel to the fuselage. This fold interlocks the two halves.

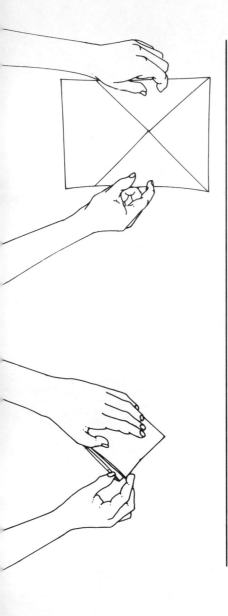

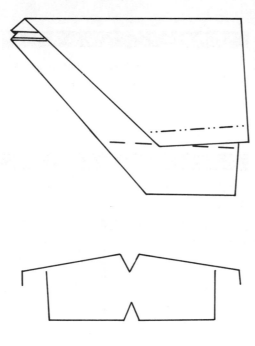

Make the winglets on the bottom section by noting where the upper wing reaches. RAT fold the upper section winglets parallel to the wing creases.

Re-establish the lower section wing folds, then set wing angles and dihedral as shown. Trim as needed. The Interlock Biplane can be easily flown in moderate winds. You'll probably need to add some up elevator on the upper wing surface. Launching can be tricky. Pinch its nose and toss like a dart, snapping your wrist on the release. Throw it level or slightly down when checking the trim. The Interlock Biplane sometimes lies on the wind similar to a box kite.

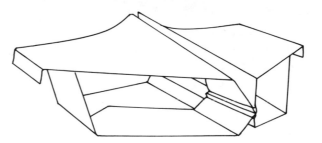

Tube

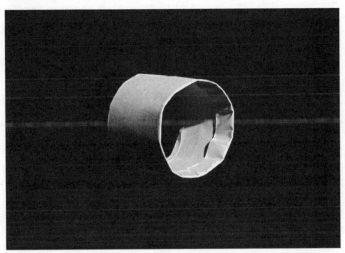

You'll get bizarre flights from this unlikely-looking plane. The tube is thrown like a football and spirals and curves its way through the air. It's easy to fold and unpredictable to fly.

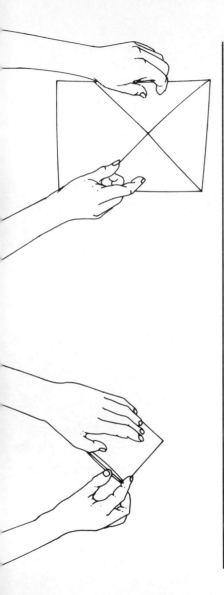

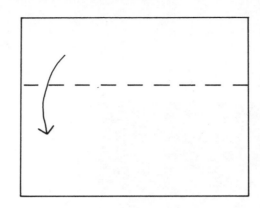

STEP 1 ◀

Fold a third of the page over. The folded portion should be the same width as the protruding, unfolded portion. It's OK for the folded portion to be a bit wider than the unfolded part, but not the other way around.

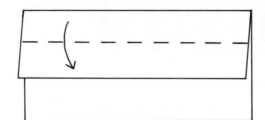

STEP 2 ◀

Fold the creased edge to the raw edge you just folded over in step 1.

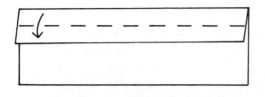

STEP 3 ▲

Fold the new creased edge to the raw edge again. With all the layers to the inside, start curving the thick part in preparation for interlocking the ends.

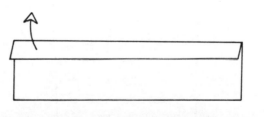

STEP 4 ▲

Unfold the crease from step 3 and slide one end inside the other as shown— about an inch and a half.

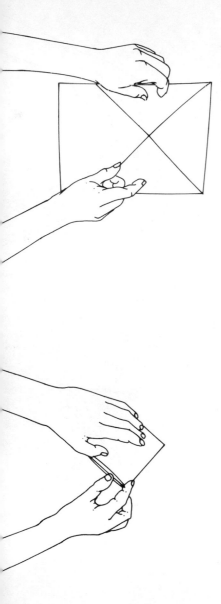

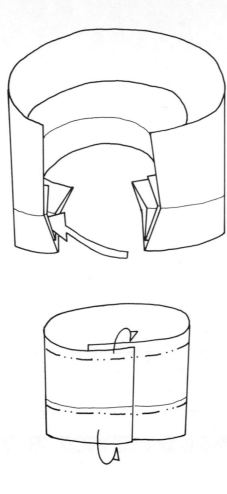

Refold the crease from step 3. This will not be easy. Some scrunching together of layers will occur, but this helps keep the tube locked together. Also make a crease on the raw edge about a quarter inch all the way around for extra help in locking the tube.

Round it out and give the Tube a toss. You'll get some weird flight patterns from this weird aircraft. Throw it like a football and watch it spiral and curve its way through the air. The only trimming needed is keeping the thing round. It's just as bizarre indoor or out, giving you loads of unpredictable fun.

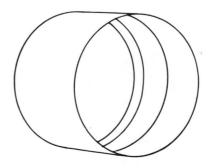

Starship Shuttle

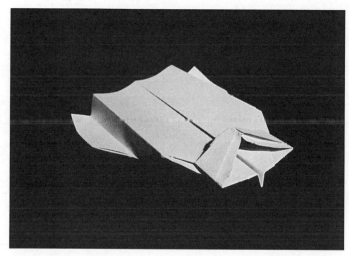

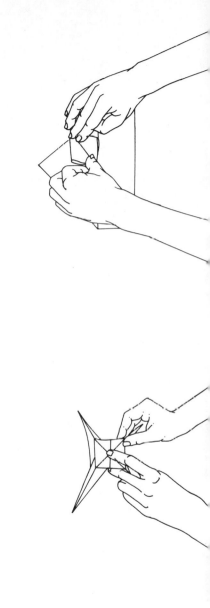

The Starship Shuttle is a good indoor glider and will perform well in low winds outdoors. Study the folding diagrams closely and you'll have no problem creating this origami airborne triumph. Its flight matches its style; it seems to ride on the air a little differently than most airplanes.

PETAL FOLD

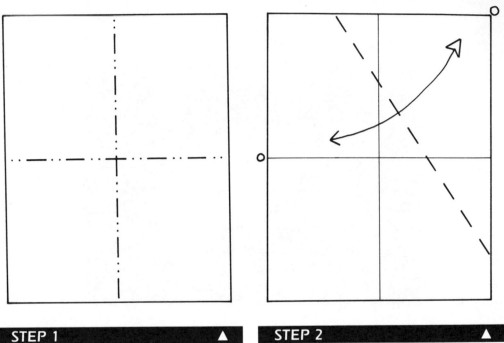

STEP 1 ▲

Mountain fold the page in half, length and width.

STEP 2 ▲

Fold the upper right corner to the center of the left edge and unfold.

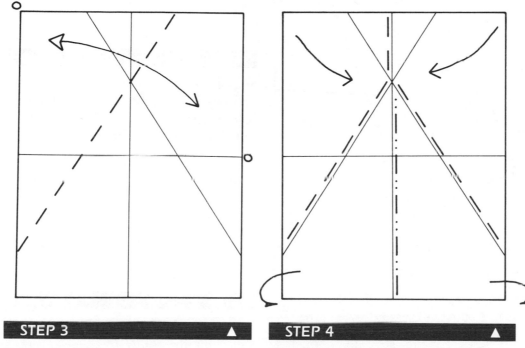

Repeat for the upper left corner.

Bring the lower corners together by mountain folding the center crease while bringing the upper corners together by valley folding the center crease. Follow the lower legs of the creases from steps 2 and 3 to accomplish this.

PETAL FOLD

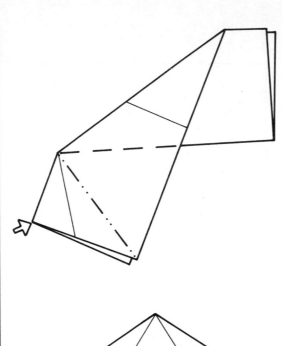

Squash fold the point. It's easier to be accurate if you make the valley folds before squashing. A squash fold is shown in the flip-through animation.

Fold up the flap with a valley fold while squashing the point.

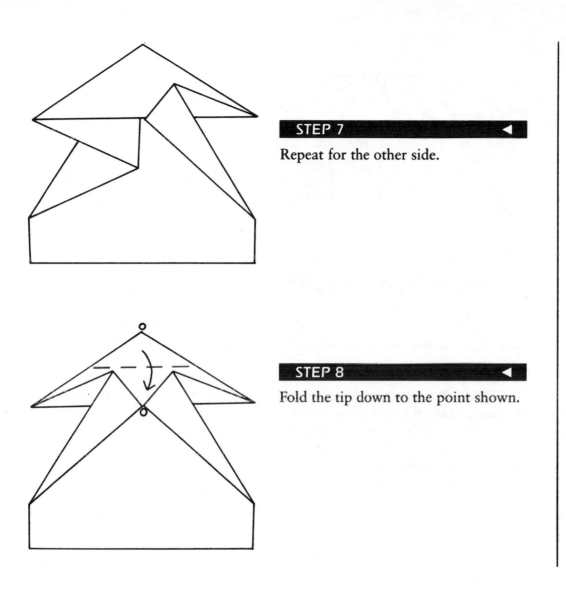

Repeat for the other side.

Fold the tip down to the point shown.

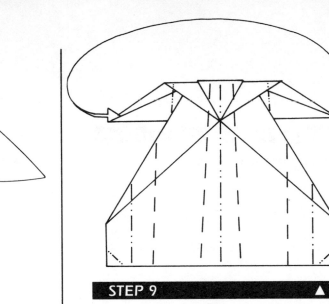

STEP 9 ▲

Here we go ... Make the main fuselage fold first. Then RAT fold the main wing parallel to the fuselage fold. Fold the raw edge of the wing to the main crease and then fold the raw edge back to the new crease. You've effectively quartered the wing. Make the cockpit assembly similar to the method used for the Trang: insert one flap inside the other, crease the center, and reverse fold part of that center crease to lock the fold. See the photo for detail. A reverse fold is shown in the flip-through animation.

Set the wing crease angles and trim as in the photos. The Starship Shuttle has a unique design often resulting in occasional barrel rolls in response to gusts of wind. Trim the corners of the wings as shown in the photos. It needs plenty of up elevator here.

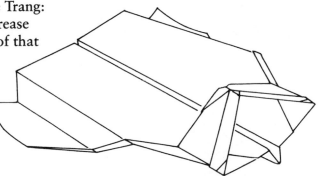

Wind Devil

The Wind Devil's special wing design keeps the airplane pointed into the wind so that it can take advantage of sudden gusts to gain altitude. It can be tricky to keep trimmed, but you won't want to pass this one up.

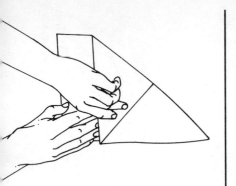

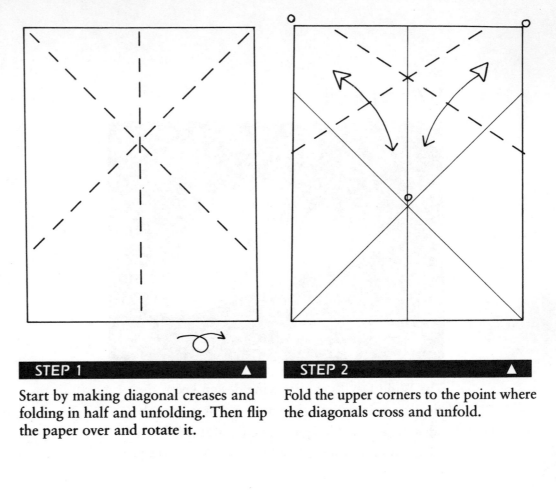

STEP 1 ▲

Start by making diagonal creases and folding in half and unfolding. Then flip the paper over and rotate it.

STEP 2 ▲

Fold the upper corners to the point where the diagonals cross and unfold.

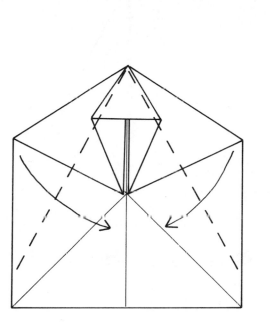

STEP 3

This is a tough fold. Make a waterbomb-like fold by following the lower legs of the creases from step 2 and placing the upper corners on the point where the lower diagonals cross. The flip-through animation shows a waterbomb base.

STEP 4

Fold the top edges to the center crease.

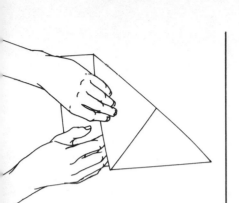

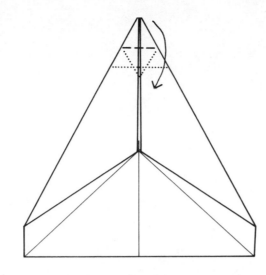

STEP 5 ▲

Fold the tip down just past the horizontal edge from step 4.

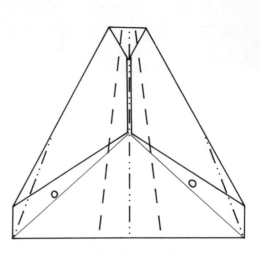

STEP 6 ▲

RAT fold the wings after folding the plane in half. A gentle slope that starts close to the fuselage fold and slopes up toward the rear will work well. The winglets need not be exactly parallel to the wing folds, but should be close. Adjust the creases marked to match the illustration of the finished plane.

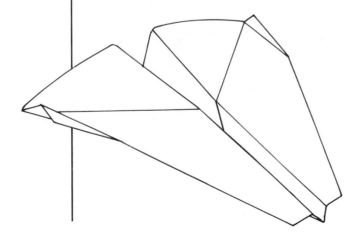

STEP 7 ◄

Set the dihedral or wing angle and trim as needed. The Wind Devil can be a devil to trim, so make the extra effort to keep the wing curvatures even for each launch.

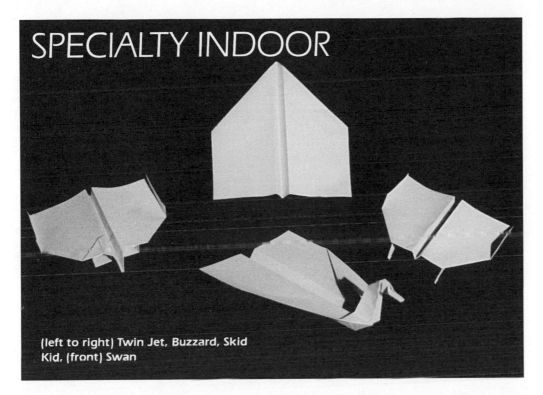

SPECIALTY INDOOR

(left to right) Twin Jet, Buzzard, Skid
Kid, (front) Swan

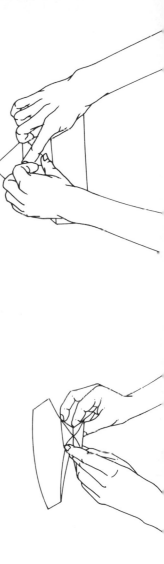

This group of aircraft flies best indoors. The Buzzard glides slowly and gracefully across a room, but can't take the unpredictable wind currents of outdoor flight; the Twin Jet is a beautiful work of origami and a respectable slow glider that performs best with a light toss. All of these aircraft are examples of the craftwork of paper airplanes, and offer a look at the possibilities of paper flight in slow motion.

Buzzard

The Buzzard is a good indoor craft with very low wing loading. It glides very slowly and gracefully, sometimes tipping slightly from side to side. It will cruise across any living room, giving the occupants plenty of time to watch. Easy to fold and fly, the Buzzard is a perfect plane for anyone stuck inside on a rainy day.

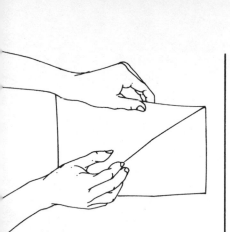

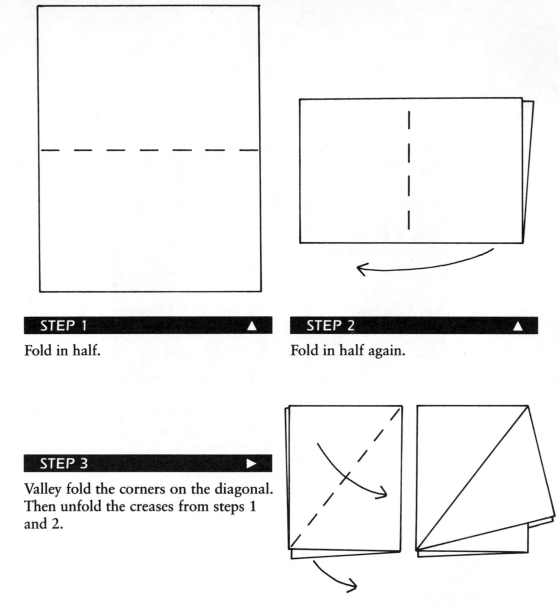

STEP 1 ▲

Fold in half.

STEP 2 ▲

Fold in half again.

STEP 3 ▶

Valley fold the corners on the diagonal.
Then unfold the creases from steps 1
and 2.

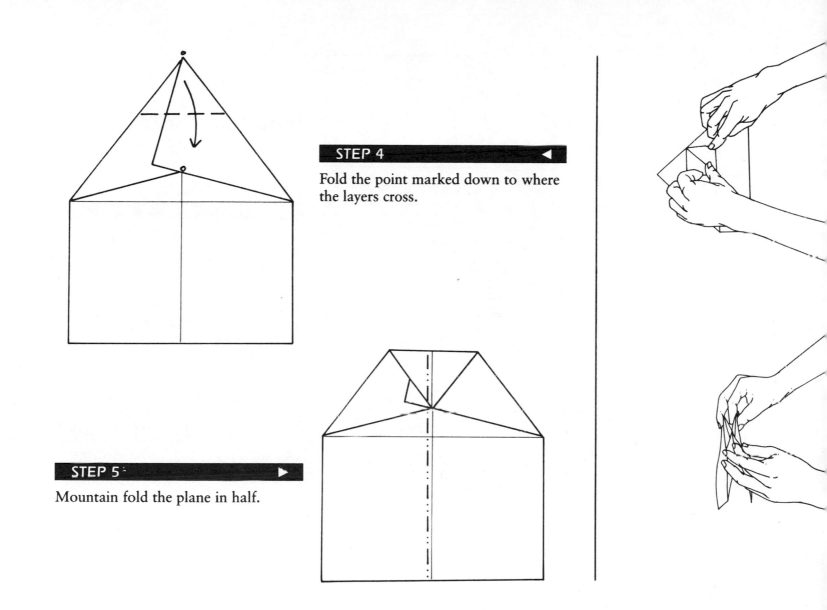

Fold the point marked down to where the layers cross.

Mountain fold the plane in half.

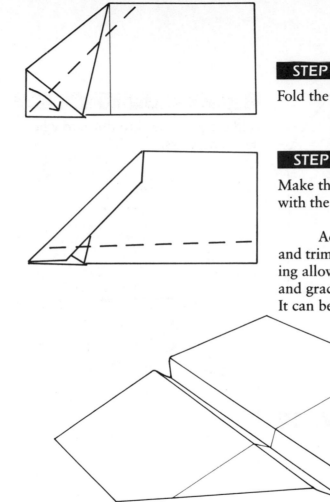

Fold the forward edge to the fuselage.

Make the wings by RAT folding parallel with the fuselage the length of the plane.

Adjust dihedral or wing angle and trim as needed. Very low wing loading allows the Buzzard to glide slowly and gracefully when properly trimmed. It can be used outdoors on only the calmest of days. Give the Buzzard a level, gentle release. It almost seems to parachute down to earth.

Twin Jet

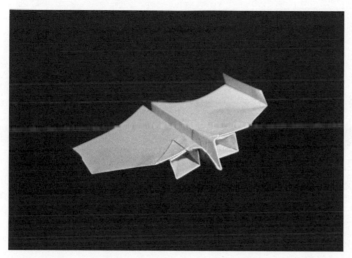

The Twin Jet is a serviceable indoor glider that when properly trimmed, will give you a smooth graceful glide. It's complex to fold and fun to watch. The Twin Jet is a must for any high-tech, indoor assault.

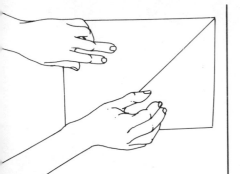

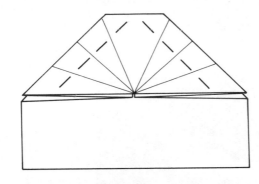

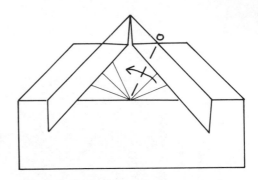

STEP 1 ▲

Fold the Trang to step 8. Then fold flaps
down so the top edge meets the center
and the creases are parallel to the edge
of each flap.

STEP 2 ▲

Fold along the existing crease. Watch
the area marked. In order to complete
this step, some bunching may occur
under the corner of this triangle.

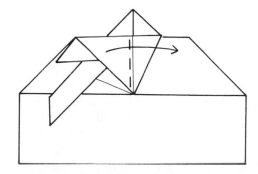

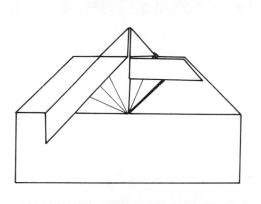

STEP 3 ▲

Fold the flap back to the right along the existing crease.

STEP 4 ▲

Repeat 2 and 3 for the left side.

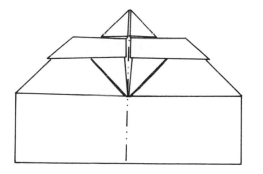

STEP 5 ◄

Mountain fold the plane in half.

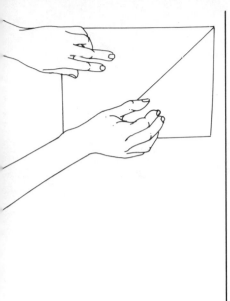

Pull the flaps down.

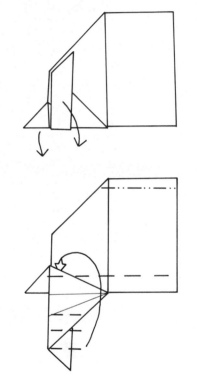

Make the two creases shown in the center of the flap first. Match them carefully with the other side. Then tuck the flap into the pocket shown; making the wing fold will hold the flap in place. RAT fold the wings so that the fuselage is about as tall as the engine creases. Make the wing crease parallel with the fuselage fold for the length of the plane. Finally, make the winglets parallel with the wing folds.

Set the dihedral or wing angle and adjust the engine creases, if needed, so that the engines match in shape and size. Trim as needed. Throw it by pinching the nose and give it a slow, slightly downward release.

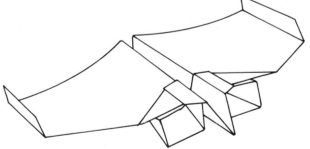

Skid Kid

The Skid Kid is a good indoor glider with special landing gear that allows it to make superb touchdowns on smooth surfaces. Hardwood floors are perfect runways, and table tops can become aircraft carrier decks. All the new folding moves are completely explained in the flip-through animation if you are a beginner. Practice landing the Skid Kid alone or compete against friends; either way you'll see how much fun getting down to earth can be.

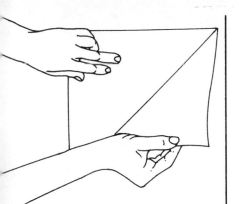

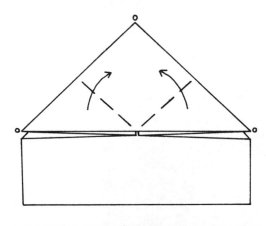

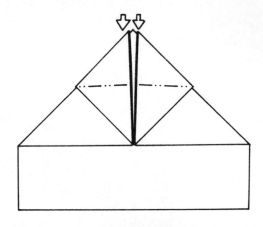

STEP 1 ▲

Make a waterbomb base and valley fold the marked points to the top. A waterbomb base is demonstrated in the flip-through animation.

STEP 2 ▲

Squash fold two points. A squash fold is shown in the flip-through animation.

STEP 3 ▶

Petal fold the two points. A petal fold is also shown in the flipthrough animation.

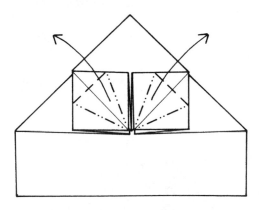

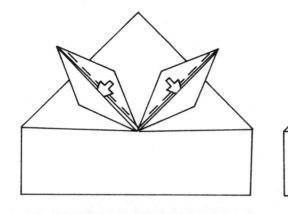

Tuck one side of the petal fold inside the other.

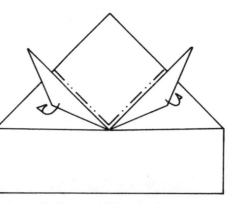

Mountain fold flaps under.

Fold the top down as far as the other layers will allow.

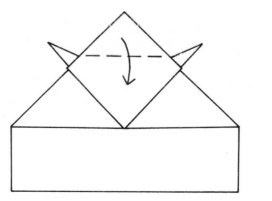

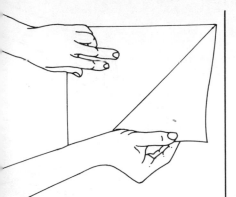

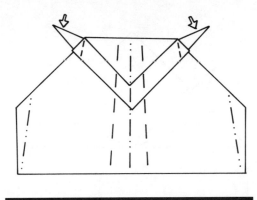

This is a synopsis of the remaining folds. Mountain fold the plane in half. Then make the wing folds RAT folds, giving you a thin fuselage that slopes up toward the rear. Make winglets and landing gear parallel with the wing folds. Finally, reverse fold the tips of the landing gear. This will help the plane skid across the floor for a smooth landing. A reverse fold is shown in the flip-through animation.

Set the dihedral or wing angle and add a slight up curve to the wings. Trim if needed.

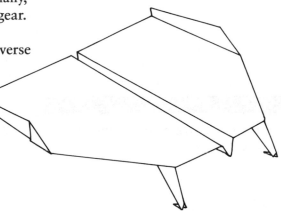

Swan

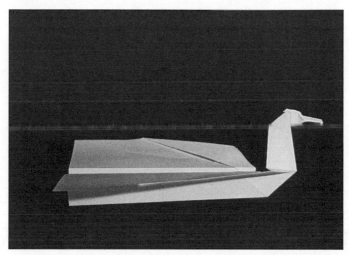

This is an indoor wonder. The Swan's performance matches its form; a great looking aircraft with a slow and even glide. It's a little harder to fold than the Phoenix, but well within the reach of beginners.

SQUASH FOLD BEGINS ON PAGE 77

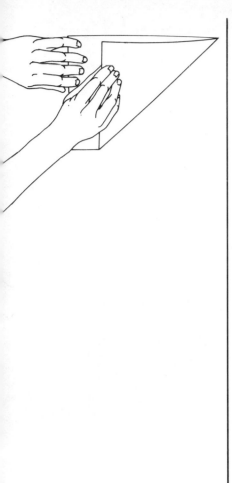

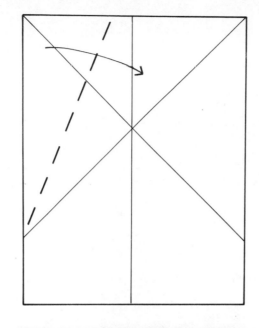

Fold and unfold diagonals and the center crease.

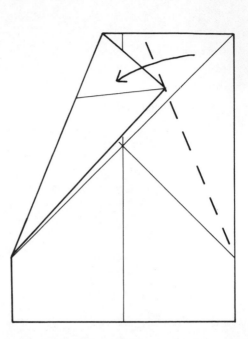

Fold the corner to the diagonal crease and line up the edge of the paper with the crease just like the Phoenix.

Make the same fold as in Step 2 for the right side.

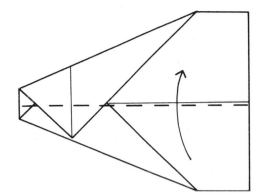

STEP 4 ◄

Fold the plane in half.

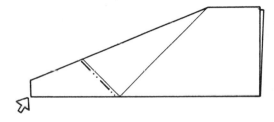

STEP 5 ◄

Reverse fold the nose along the existing creases. A reverse fold is shown in the flip-through animation.

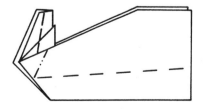

STEP 6 ◄

The wing fold is RAT fold that has a very gentle slope up as it nears the tail. You pull the wing down as you narrow the neck. Repeat for the other wing.

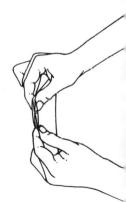

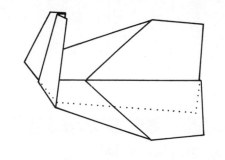

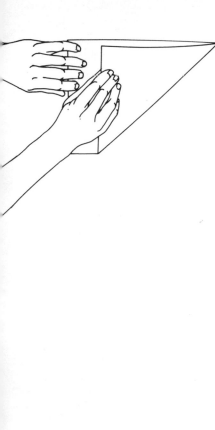

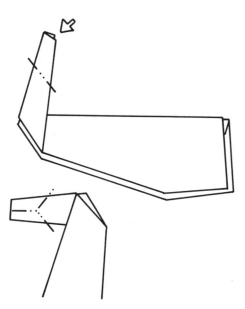

STEP 7 ▲

Reverse fold about here to create the head.

STEP 8 ▶

Pinch the Swan's bill into shape.

STEP 9 ▼

Set dihedral and trim as needed.

The Swan should fly slowly and gracefully with a minimum of adjustment. It's a limited use glider, but a great looking one. Wing angle should be fairly flat as in the illustration.

ACCESSORIES

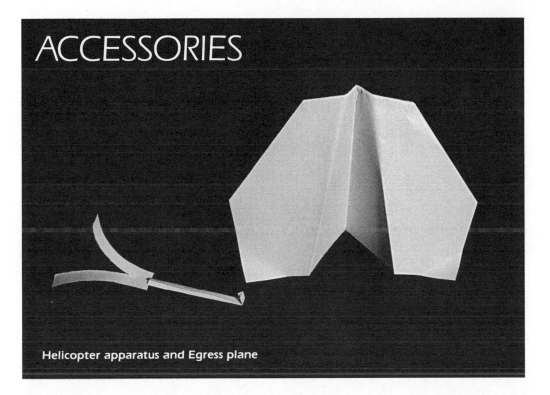

Helicopter apparatus and Egress plane

This is where it gets serious. Operating any of these systems in public may result in a collective shaking of heads. Here are the extras with which only devoted flyers of paper airplanes get involved. The Catapult, the rigging for Kites, and the Egress system are not for the timid. The accessories were developed because of the sturdiness of most of the designs in this book; the planes demanded different launching and flying systems. Enter these pages and forfeit your amateur status.

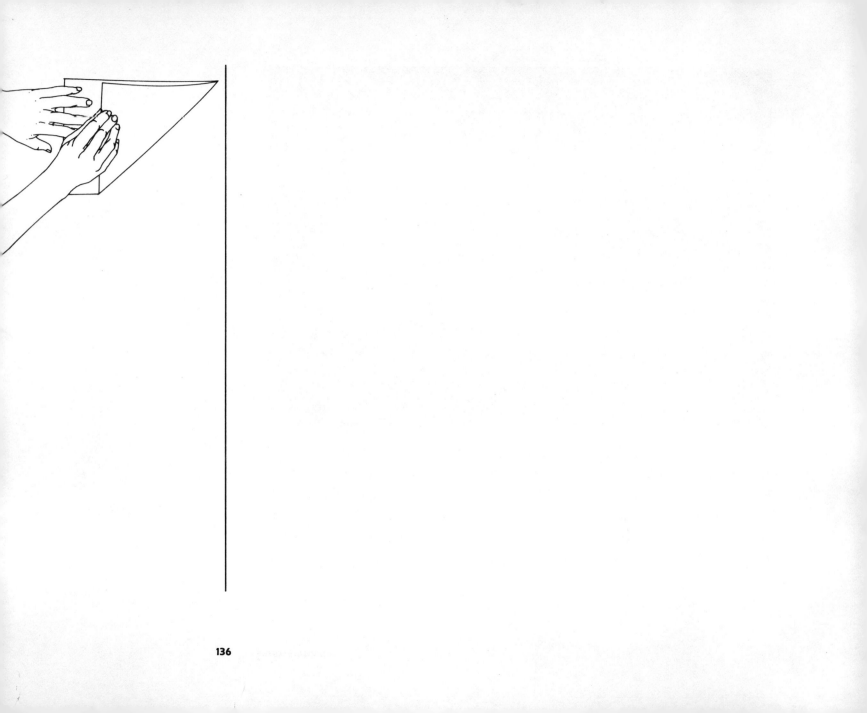

The Catapult Launch

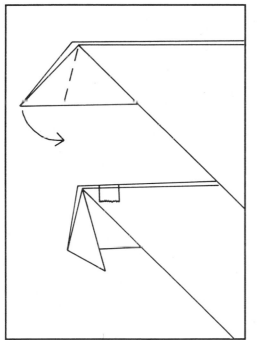

This is the easiest of the accessories to master. Some airplanes have a protruding nose. For those designs, simply outside-reverse-fold the nose to form a hook. Then tape the fuselage shut at the nose.

The rubber band can be stretched between thumb and forefinger, or you

can build a simple system as shown, using a small stick. Chopsticks are excellent.

I recommend the Stealth for this method of launch. It's a sturdy airplane that will hold up under the abuse.

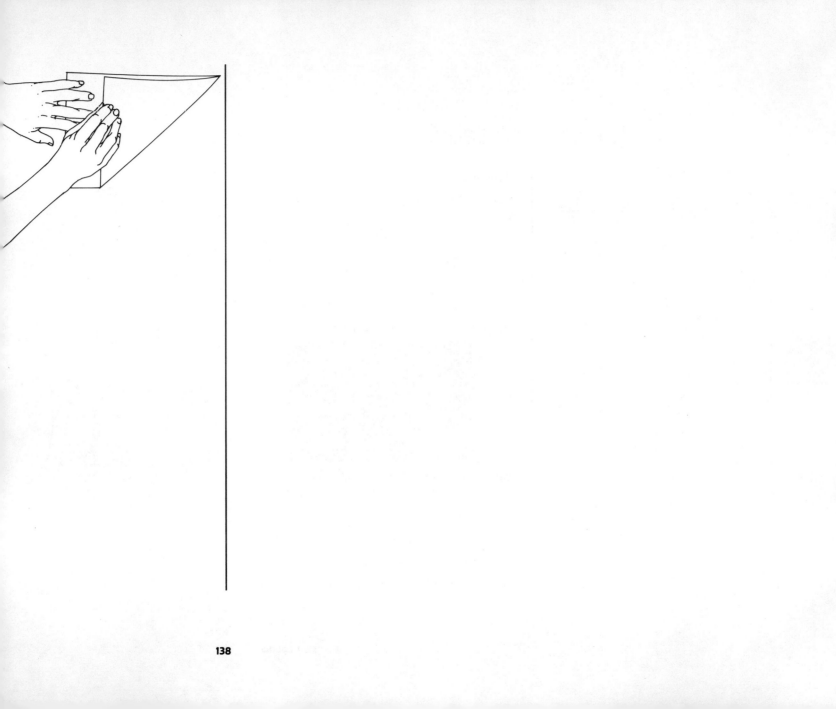

138

The Helicopter Egress System

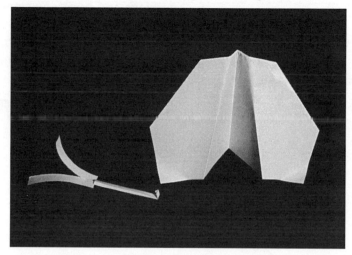

The airplane shown here was designed specifically for this mission, but you can modify most of the airplanes in the book for looping or rolling. The important thing to modify is the fuselage so that it will flop open in flight. Alternately flatten and refold the fuselage crease concentrating on the nose of the plane, where there are the most layers of paper. This will allow the fuselage to flop open at the correct time, dropping the payload.

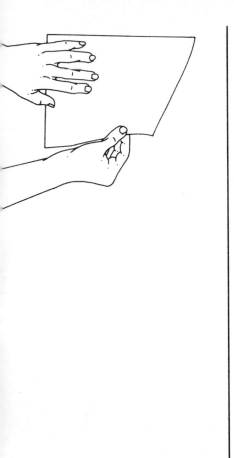

Fold up the plane, loosen the fuselage, and trim for looping or rolling. The two diagrams show you how—extra up for looping or bend just one wing as shown for rolling. Insert the helicopter into the fuselage and hook the small bent part over the nose. You're ready to throw.

Throwing and trimming must work together for this stunt to work.

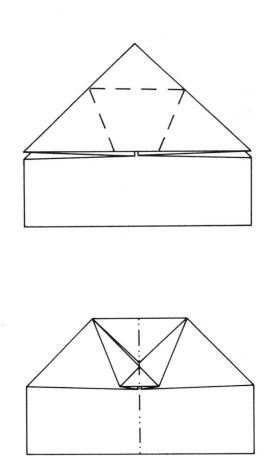

STEP 1 ◄

Start with a waterbomb base; the flip-through animation shows you how. Fold the outside corners as you would an origami paper cup. The fold the top point down over them.

STEP 2 ◄

Fold the plane in half.

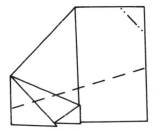

Trim for looping

STEP 3 ◀

Make a wing fold by starting about a half to ¾ of an inch above the fuselage crease and folding like the Phoenix. Add in a large amount of up elevator to make the aircraft loop.

STEP 3A ◀

For lower ceilings, trim the plane for rolling by folding only one wing tip down as shown. You still crease the main wing as shown in step 3.

SINK FOLD BEGINS ON PAGE 35

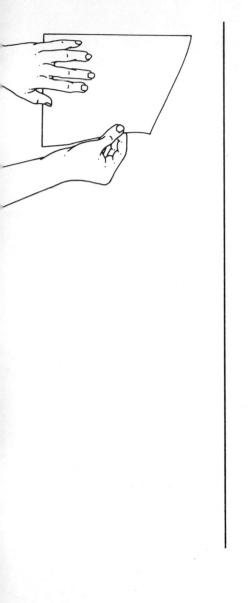

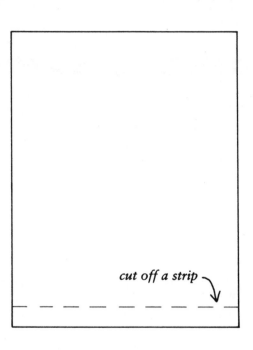

cut off a strip

STEP 4 ◄

To make the helicopter, cut a strip of paper about ¾ to ⅞ of an inch wide off the bottom of an 8½ by 11 sheet.

STEP 5 ▶

The thin dashed lines are cuts. Fold over approximately ⅓ of the strip. Cut down the center of the other end leaving some room between the end of the cut and folded layers. Make two small cuts about ⅓ of the way through from either side.

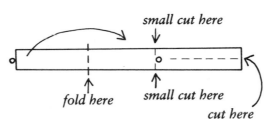

small cut here

fold here   *small cut here*

cut here

STEP 6 ▶

Fold together as shown putting one side on top of the other.

STEP 7 ▶

Fold a small portion of the bottom up. Spread the blades apart and give them a slight curve as in the illustrations.

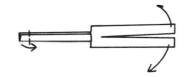

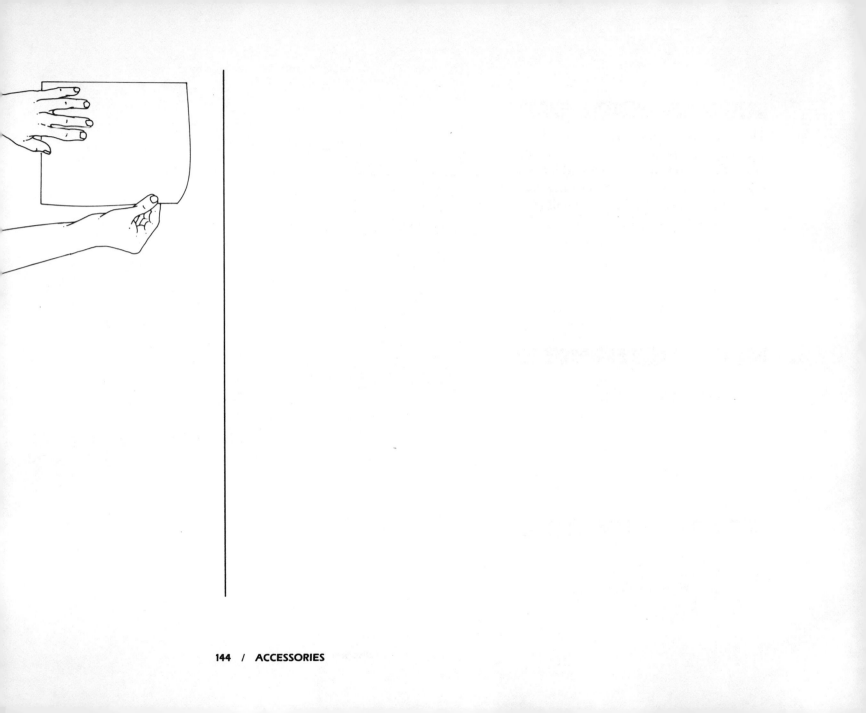

Kites

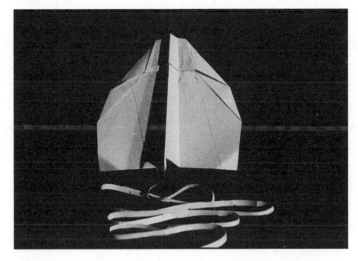

For the single control line system, use two loops
of thread. Thread a needle and push it through the
upper holes. Give yourself plenty of slack and tie
off the loop. Next, tape the rear of the fuselage as
shown. Then pinch the fuselage together and run the
needle through it, making the lower holes shown.
Give yourself some slack and tie off a loop. Tie or
tape the two loops together so that the bridle looks

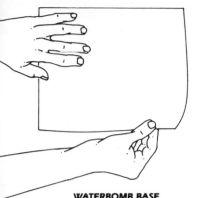

WATERBOMB BASE

like the picture. Center the connection over the fuselage and tape the thread in place on the top side of the airplane. Tie on the control line and add a tail. The tail should be at least three ¼ inch wide strips of the same paper of which you made the plane. Or you can use a long strip of newspaper.

If you feel that the bridle is adjusted correctly and the kite still spins left or right, add more tail and try trimming in a serious amount of up elevator.

For dual control line flying make the loops by using an upper and lower hold on either side for each. Connect each loop to a control line so that the bridle takes the shape shown in the drawing. The tail specifications are the same as single control line.

You'll be figure-eighting your airplane/kite in no time at all.

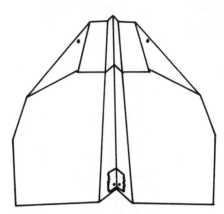

The underside of the Plane.

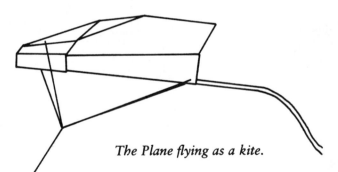

The Plane flying as a kite.